HAPPILY
Forever
AFTER

HAPPILY *forever* AFTER

KIM A. NELSON

DESERET
BOOK

SALT LAKE CITY, UTAH

Library of Congress Cataloging-in-Publication Data

Nelson, Kim A.
   Happily Forever After / Kim A. Nelson.
     p.   cm.
   ISBN 1-59038-217-X (cloth)
   1. Marriage—United States.   2. Communication in marriage—United States.   3. Marriage—Religious aspects—United States.   4. Man–Woman relationships—United States.   I. Title.

HQ734.N4213   2004
646.7'8—dc22   2003025000

Printed in the United States of America   72076-7163
Publishers Printing, Salt Lake City, UT

10   9   8   7   6   5   4   3   2   1

To Lois—my wife, my companion, my friend.

Contents

Part 3:
Skills: Making the Possible Real

Acknowledgments

ois and I have made it a lifelong habit to search out the heroes that surround us. These heroes in our lives have been those who exemplified qualities we seek to develop or improve. We would like to acknowledge some of those couples who have helped us see the forever possibilities in marriage.

Our friends Gordon and Myrna are always kind to each other and show mutual respect. They are the king and queen of appropriate public marital behavior. I know them well enough to testify that their private time reflects the same feelings and behavior. Don and Jane generously reach out and offer an inclusive spirit of love. They are tireless in their support for each other and their children. We have observed the examples of many people successfully striving to be married. Steve and Janet, Ann and Dale, Susan and Darren, Trevin and Nicole, Hank and Victoria, April and Gary, JD and Sue,

Cary and Jeanne, Andy and Janet—these and others are our proof sources that the world still holds heroes.

Special thanks to those who have read manuscripts, given encouragement, and made suggestions. Bill Phillips, Don Swartz, Sarah Nelson, Rebecca Mumm, Rachel Johnson, Chanda Hair, Jack Lyon, Chris Schoebinger, and many others.

Finally, special thanks to my friend and brother Stephen E. Robinson, who encouraged me to begin this project, and to Emily Watts, that blessing wrapped in talent, for her editing and care.

Thank you all.

PART 1

Commitment: Embracing the Possibilities

Chapter 1

What Is This Book?

I find the great thing in this world is not so much where we stand, as in what direction we are moving: To reach the port of heaven, we must sail sometimes with the wind and sometimes against it, but we must sail, and not drift, nor lie at anchor.

—*Oliver Wendell Holmes*

On a large, city car lot are two identical cars. Alike in every detail, they are delivered to their new owners. Then, four years later, the cars are returned to the dealer for appraisal. Are the cars still of equal value?

Most likely the cars that began as identical twins have different value now. What makes the difference? How they were treated, where they have been, who has cared for them and how—these and a hundred other variables. One of the cars may now be junk, ready for the scrap heap. The other may have become a classic, almost beyond value. But without exception, cars that have been well maintained and cared for are the ones of most worth.

That is how our marriages are. Well protected, carefully steered, properly maintained and cared for, they can become classics in every sense. Our marriages can be a pleasure to be in, dependable and effective in even the most hazardous conditions. They will transport and protect us if we have properly prepared them for the job.

How we care for our marriages adds tangible value to our lives. If we really want to improve, grow, and share an eternal relationship, we must learn all we can about the principles and skills that make that possible. In practical terms, that means a lifetime of study, communication, and practice. The joyful truth is that the process is part of the product. As we live our lives, we can find value and happiness in every growing day. The importance we place on our marriage will be obvious to us, our families, and anyone who observes it. That obvious interest proclaims our conviction that our marriage is worth the effort.

Learning the Process

Imagine for a moment that you and your spouse have been invited to spend an evening playing games with friends. Your friends have discovered a new game that they have played several times, and they've been telling you what fun it is—in fact, you've heard about this game from several of your friends who have tried it. You don't know how to play, but by agreeing to join the game, you have signified your willingness to make the effort to learn the rules and abide by them.

Because you are new and want to learn the game well enough to enjoy playing it, you are extra observant. If you're lucky, someone you trust will help you along, but at the very least, you can watch the more experienced players. They begin by teaching you the basics. If they are good teachers and you are good students, there is the promise of some real fun ahead. You keep trying, getting better with practice, and as you improve, you see the potential for further success. What was at first foreign and difficult becomes easier. You develop strategies and theories about how to get better at the game. You begin each new session more experienced and more familiar with the ins and outs of playing. With luck and effort, you continue to be more successful and have more fun.

Even the most expert players may at times interpret the rules differently or forget some nuance. Then the players consult the rule book and perhaps do some negotiating to reach an agreement about how to play. Sometimes, as players become even more proficient, they agree on new interpretations of the rules that make the game even more exciting and fun. In effect, experienced players customize the game. They make changes in order to better accommodate their specific skills and goals.

A couple's commitment to be married is something like that imaginary game. The promise of a rewarding and mutually enjoyable experience moves us to commit to participate long before we know all the "rules." Our commitment is based on the promise of what lies ahead. We don't expect perfection, but we do expect to enjoy the process and to get better at it as time goes on. Because of that expectation, we commit to learn, to be observant, to practice and improve. We learn with every experience how to be better. We consult expert players and other available resources to improve our skill and understanding. We develop our own theories, and with luck and practice the game gets easier and much more fun. We may never be perfect players, but we can enjoy the challenge and process of improving.

Improving the quality of our relationships, specifically our marriages, improves our lives and the lives of our children, extended families, co-workers, fellow volunteers, and communities. In short, happier and healthier people are the building blocks of a happier world.

Our Father in Heaven endorses marriage. In Doctrine and Covenants 49:15 the Lord proclaims, "Verily I say unto you, that whoso forbiddeth to marry is not ordained of God, for marriage is ordained of God unto man." And in "The Family: A Proclamation to the World," the First Presidency and Quorum of the Twelve have written, "Husband and wife have a solemn responsibility to love and care for each other and for their children." The same document later asserts, "The family is ordained of God. Marriage between man and woman is essential to His eternal plan." God loves us and wants only the best for each of us. We are social creatures, intended to live in community, and the most basic community is the marriage relationship. That is true in this world and the next. It follows, then, that a godly marriage offers the best way of living, not only for both partners but also for each spouse as an individual. Understanding this truth is fundamental to our personal happiness.

WHAT THIS BOOK IS—AND WHAT IT ISN'T

This is a book for those who are married or have an interest in marriage. My hope is to provide a practical guide for couples and individuals who want to learn, grow, or heal. The key words here are *practical* and *want*. The work to do is here if you choose to do it.

The case studies and examples I have used are illustrative, and the names and specific details are in some cases changed to protect the confidential nature of past relationships. In the cases where people are referred to by their real names, permission was given for the reference.

You don't need to be in big marital trouble to benefit from the ideas presented in this book. That would be like assuming you must have a wreck before you can benefit from driver's education. The goal is not to salvage a mess but to avoid one by having the very best growing, living, celestial marriage possible. That said, if you have a mess going, you can get to work and salvage it. The objective in either case is the same: to have the best relationship possible.

A great relationship requires hard work, courage, and strength. Consider the teaching of the Chinese sage

Lao Tsu: "To be deeply loved by someone gives you strength; to deeply love someone gives you courage."

The goals for marriage that we will discuss in this book may at first seem miles away, impossible to reach. Don't panic! The trick is to focus on improving, on moving from where you are now in the direction of where you want to be. The starting point, wherever it is for you at this time, is not the main issue.

The objective is for the information here to be interesting and useable. A lot of what you read will seem familiar. Things that make sense almost always do. Remember the popular book by Robert Fulghum, *All I Really Need to Know I Learned in Kindergarten*? What made the book and title so interesting to me was how it pointed out the power of simple truths applied. I have found that there is much wisdom in what we choose to teach children. The clearest and most useful concepts are the ones we give to those we love the most. If you have any questions about what you read here or find elsewhere, or about how to use it, practice what we teach our children: search, ponder, and pray.

This book can be used as a ready reference source for concepts, principles, strategies, and even exercises to help build your marriage relationship. From time to time an exercise is provided to help you apply the information to your own circumstances. If the idea of an exercise is too structured for you or your spouse, you may want to simply discuss the concepts together. If so, a description of possible discussion ideas is also provided along with each exercise. We all learn and retain information differently, so do what works best for you. My goal is to provide helpful, applicable information in enough ways to make it useable.

Now that you know what this book is, may I offer one small caution as to what it is *not*. Nothing in this book is meant to be used as an "I-told-you-so" club with which to beat your spouse. Even if some of what you read might seem perfect for pointing out to your mate, "See, I was right" or "It says right here that if you don't do it the way I've been trying to tell you, you're wrong," using the information in that way would be counterproductive, defeating the intended purpose. What you find here can't work as a tool for building your marriage if you try to make it a weapon for destroying it at the same time.

Instead, let your husband or wife discover with you how something included here might be of value. The example you set by learning and growing gives others around you permission to do the same. If they see you benefit from what you are learning, they are more likely to try it themselves.

Our relationships need different emphases at different times. Building blocks such as communication, education, and other things we'll be discussing in this book all have great value, but we need to remember, in sharing them, the lesson of the stone mason. Suppose you are building a wonderful house and want to use a particular piece of building material. You know it is good material, but it just doesn't fit right now. That does *not* mean that the material is bad or that the project is flawed. All it means is that the time is wrong for that piece. It may not fit now, but it will at some point.

The same is true for the information in this book. If a concept is not working for you, set it aside; the application will come when the environment is correct. Don't worry about trying to force a square peg into a round hole; if it is a good peg, have faith that there will be some square holes on the horizon. For example, later we will discuss the value of holding a weekly planning and scheduling meeting to improve family management and communication with your spouse. This requires the commitment of both spouses to meet weekly to coordinate calendars and plan the week's activities. Perhaps you and your spouse don't have a lot of outside demands on the family schedule. If you don't yet have children, you might already be discussing upcoming events over a quiet dinner every night. In that case, the scheduling meeting might seem redundant.

Remember, however, that your circumstances may change in the future. There may be new employment or church callings, and the addition of music lessons, soccer games, basketball, or other activities that come with the changing makeup of your family might make the weekly coordination of schedules some of the most valuable time you spend together.

Marriage is God's plan for eternity. It is part of becoming more like Him, knowing the things He knows, experiencing a fullness of eternal joy. That's a pretty lofty expression of the desired outcome, especially for people not even sure they have the strength or even the desire to make it through the day.

However, looking forward to the goal of eternal joy is a hopeful thing. Hope, not happiness, is the opposite of depression. Every hopeful moment in our lives is positive. Things will not always go perfectly. Not every moment can be fun or happy. But every hopeful moment is a promise of the future we seek. In hope, we discover a grand key to making that future happen. Perhaps that's what this book is really about. Perhaps discovering such a key is what marriage is really about.

CHAPTER 2

What Kind of Marriage Do You Want?

Many persons have the wrong idea about what constitutes true happiness. It's not attained through self-gratification but through fidelity to a worthy purpose.
—Helen Keller

What type of marriage do we choose to have? There are many types of marriage, but I have noticed three that I would like to discuss. Each is easily recognizable and familiar as we look around us.

The first is parasitic. A parasite is one organism living off another, deriving its sustenance from the strength of the other and offering no benefit in return. Not only is no benefit offered in return, but most parasites also harm the host.

Cancer is parasitic. It devours, consumes, and even kills the body it inhabits—a body that was healthy without it! There are various kinds of parasites, but the one thing they share is a universal disregard for the host organism.

"What's in it for me?" is the defining question asked by the parasite. Parasitic marriages are highly destructive to the people in them. These are partnerships that destroy the partners in the most dramatic and obvious ways.

Whenever I think of this type of relationship, I'm tempted to look at the parasite and blame him or her and see the host as a powerless victim. In truth, both are victims and neither is powerless. The ultimate loss by both parties in a parasitic relationship is illustrated in a favorite quotation from Mahatma Gandhi, referring to the colonial rule of India by Great Britain. Speaking to the British people he said, "We will not submit to this injustice—not merely because it's destroying us but because it's destroying you as well."

The Mahatma was obviously aware that, in the long run, parasitic relationships are mutually destructive. He also recognized his right and the right of his people to refuse to submit to being devoured.

It's up to the host to refuse to submit to the parasite. As with fighting a disease, we must first identify it and then seek help, if necessary, to find the cure, a way to rid ourselves of the parasite's destructive power.

This model is an illustration of what must unfortunately be done in parasitic relationships. For example, a physically abusive spouse must never be tolerated. Other forms of parasitic behaviors include addictions of many kinds—gambling, drugs, sexual addictions, and so forth.

Other more subtle examples of this type of relationship include the trophy wife who serves as window dressing in her husband's career, or the source-of-income husband whose only role is to provide money for his wife. There are hundreds of other variations on the theme, but the pattern is the same: one provides, the other consumes.

Even though we may love the person who behaves in these ways, we must exercise our agency by not participating in this type of relationship. As Gandhi so beautifully states, it's wrong not only because it will destroy us but because it will destroy them as well.

The Little Bird and the Rhino

The second and most common type of marriage is the symbiotic relationship. Symbiosis is the commonly used term for what is more accurately called mutualism. *Symbiosis* as we use it here is a relationship where partners coexist in order to receive mutual benefit.

This partnership is one we might have first been made aware of in high school biology class when we learned about that little bird that lives in the ear of a rhinoceros. Mr. Baird, my teacher, described it like this: The bird eats ticks and other bothersome insects and warns of approaching danger. The rhino has bad eyesight and needs the warning of the bird, and the rhino enjoys being rid of the insects. The bird gets a home high enough off the ground to avoid some predators, and it enjoys the companionship of a combination mobile home and food source.

This sounds pleasant enough and is certainly better than a parasitic relationship. Extended to marriage, this is actually a maintenance relationship. It may be convenient, useful, and even pleasant. It is not, however, the partnership that God intended to bring us a fullness of joy.

Clearly, this kind of relationship might be a functional way to live. I'll trade my skills and assets for yours. You cook and I'll buy the food. We share a house and have someone to attend the office Christmas party with. We experience occasional sexual release and have someone to split driving the kids around with. It works. The key seems to be keeping score in such a way that we're sure we each get our respective 50 percent out of the deal.

Some of the marriages that end up here were never intended by the couple to be this way. They just got here because this is the marriage our world leads us to. This is the arrangement that represents the efficient, routine, business partnership. I serve my self-interest and contribute my fair share, and so do you. This type of marriage consists of two independent people living together in a mutually beneficial way.

The result of this kind of arrangement is two separate people who never really receive the benefit of becoming one with each other or—in partnership—with the Lord. A close friend described her version of the maintenance marriage this way: "I'm so afraid of what will happen when our last child leaves home. There we'll be, together in that big house, with nothing to do and nothing in common."

The tragedy here is not just the bleak future of this partnership but also the obviously wasted years. How much joy and growth was missed because you and I never paid the price to be us. Another friend described his dilemma this way: "When I retire, I want a rest. I would like to go fishing, read, and go for some long walks. My wife says she is so afraid of having me around with nothing to do that she hopes I never retire." In other words, "Things are fine as long as we don't have to be together."

Is it any wonder that so many of our children are asking—after they observe this type of relationship, the relationship of the world—"Why even bother with marriage?" The appropriate response is, don't. Not for this kind of marriage. Set your sights higher.

WHAT COULD BE OURS

The third type of relationship is a celestial marriage. It is the relationship we've been describing so far as our goal. The objective is a marriage relationship worth the effort. The celestial relationship is that partnership described by the Lord in Matthew 19:5–6: "For this cause shall a man leave father and mother, and shall cleave to his wife: and they twain shall be one flesh. Wherefore they are no more twain, but one flesh. What therefore

God hath joined together, let not man put asunder." And in Ephesians 5:21, that relationship is described like this: "Submitting yourselves one to another in the fear of God."

These two scriptures mention two of the keys to having a celestial marriage. First, man and wife are no longer two but one flesh. There's no keeping score. As individuals we're members of a team so closely identified with each other that what's good or bad for one is good or bad for the other. This is the Christlike charity that defines a celestial marriage, recognizing what is good for *us*.

Second, "submitting" yourself means giving up pride, but without submitting mindlessly to slavery. That means humbly, willingly, and with full awareness contributing all you have to your marriage. In this type of union we willingly give up all competing affections and loyalties. We become true partners holding nothing back "just in case this doesn't work out."

I'm reminded of the story of a little girl who kept falling out of bed. Exasperated, her parents finally took her to a doctor for help. After a careful examination, finding no medical reason for her problem, the doctor asked, "Why do you keep falling out of bed?"

The little girl considered the question and then replied, "I guess I just sleep too close to where I got into bed."

She discovered a great truth. We need to get all the way in if we plan on staying in safely.

The current politically correct interpretation of submission in a relationship has become synonymous with defeat or slavery. What we are talking about is neither. It is the process of living up to a two-way commitment made of our own free will and choice. It is honoring the potential of the union and giving value to the agreement that we made to create it.

The value the Lord places on submission to the marriage promise is clearly stated in Ephesians. The vow of husband and wife, submitting to and loving each other, values the unity of couple above self. The direction for husband and wife to give all they have to the other is given with the clear requirement that both husband and wife are worthy to receive such a gift.

Ephesians 5:21–25 says, "[Submit] yourselves one to another in the fear of God. Wives, submit yourselves unto your own husbands, as unto the Lord. For the husband is the head of the wife, even as Christ is the head of the church: and he is the saviour of the body. Therefore as the church is subject unto Christ, so let the wives be to their own husbands in every thing. Husbands, love your wives, even as Christ also loved the church, and gave himself for it."

It's a fortunate wife who has a husband willing to give his life for her. And a husband who has a wife worthy of such a sacrifice is just as blessed. If we are willing to give these big things for our spouses, can we not also give daily the small gifts that demonstrate this level of commitment?

This is the kind of love that promises to care for us even if we get sick, for such care lifts and blesses us both. This is the level of commitment that transcends our time together here on earth and enters eternity as a component of how we measure our future together. This is a relationship defined by faith, hope, and charity, and "whoso is found possessed of it at the last day, it shall be well with him" (Moroni 7:47).

The unfeigned love you have for yourself and for your mate is the power that can carry you beyond a poor or even average relationship to a celestial one. By expressing this love, you have, without thought of reward, extended yourself to another. That is charity. It is that sweet, pure feeling we all recognize when it comes our way.

My first remembered experience with real charity came from my grandma. It didn't matter what she was doing or whom she was with; when I came to her front door, I was welcome. Not only was she happy to see me, but she also made sure I knew it. This was not a big thing, certainly not an earth-shattering event, but it made me feel great. I suppose you would not be surprised to know that, though it has been many years since her passing, my Grandma Kinghorn still has my heart. Such is the power of real charity. It's the only power available to help lift another person.

Every time we exercise true charity, every time we willingly extend ourselves for the purpose of nurturing our own or another's spiritual growth, we benefit. We come closer to understanding our Father's and the Savior's love for us than at almost any other time, for in that moment of charity, we are like them. We feel their love as we love others and ourselves.

Loving, as most of us already understand, can be a difficult, even arduous task. It can also fill us with grace and hope and purity. Consider these words from Mormon and Paul as they speak of the great gifts that come from God's kind of love:

"Charity suffereth long, and is kind, and envieth not, and is not puffed up, seeketh not her own, is not easily provoked, thinketh no evil, and rejoiceth not in iniquity but rejoiceth in the truth, beareth all things, believeth all things, hopeth all things, endureth all things. . . . Charity is the pure love of Christ, and it endureth forever; and whoso is found possessed of it at the last day, it shall be well with him" (Moroni 7:45, 47).

"Though I speak with the tongues of men and of angels, and have not charity, I am become as sounding brass, or a tinkling cymbal. . . . And now abideth faith, hope, charity, these three; but the greatest of these is charity" (1 Corinthians 13:1, 13).

WHERE CAN THIS LOVE TAKE US?

I am indebted to M. Scott Peck for a very good working definition of love from his book *The Road Less Traveled*. He has recognized rightly a truth we all know innately—that love of self is a necessary part of loving others. Dr. Peck says:

What is this force that pushes us as individuals and as a whole species to grow against the natural resistance of our own lethargy? We have already labeled it. It is love. *Love was defined as "the will to extend one's self for the purpose of nurturing one's own or another's spiritual growth."* When we grow, it's because we are working at it. And we're working at it because we love ourselves. It is through love that we elevate ourselves. And it is through our love of others that we assist others to elevate themselves. It is evolution in progress. The evolutionary force present in all life manifests itself in mankind as human love. Among humanity, love is the miraculous force that defies the natural law of entropy. ([New York: Simon & Schuster, 1978], 268.)

The impact of this kind of love is far-reaching, recognized widely for its power to help and heal. Charitable love is not mindless submission to another or complete sacrifice of self. It is recognizing our potential to contribute to the quality of life, not only for others but also for ourselves.

A celestial marriage is what we should set our sights on. The good news is, it is within our grasp!

CHAPTER 3

The Only Person You Can Change Is You

Courage is resistance to fear, mastery of fear—not absence of fear.
—*Mark Twain*

*O*ne concept that needs to be understood before we can embark safely on the process of building a marriage is this: By definition, marriage means two people, and you control only one of them.

This proves problematic—even painful—for many. But it's the truth: The only person you can control is you. You can't change, modify, force, compel, or constrain anyone but yourself.

This leads to one inevitable conclusion: The only part of the relationship that you control is your part.

Now, you might ask, "Why is this one of the first subjects in a book about relationships?" The answer is simple. Misunderstanding this profound principle is, in my opinion, the single most significant cause of marital pain. Unbelievable as it might seem, I can love my partner with all my heart; serve her hand and foot; never miss a birthday or anniversary; and bring her cards, candy, and flowers every day—and she can still choose not to love or even like me.

The flip side is also true. Lois, my near-perfect wife, often loves me in spite of my actions as a husband rather than because of them. She *chooses* to love me. This has as much or more to do with who *she* is as with who *I* am.

Don't get me wrong. I think that someone who is a kind, loving marriage partner has a much better chance of being happily engaged in a successful, long-term relationship than a person who is not loving or sensitive. The point, though, is that it takes two people participating to have a relationship.

CONNECTING THE DOTS

Try this illustration. Make a single dot on a clean piece of paper. Now make another single dot anywhere else on the paper. These two marks, these dots, now have a relationship. They can be described in relation to each other. They can get closer or farther apart. They can move all over the page together or separately. But as long as both choose to stay on the same page, there is a relationship.

Now erase one dot. No matter how the remaining dot moves about the page, wishes it moved, or stays perfectly still, there is no other dot with which to have a relationship. In practical terms, without both dots being willingly on the same page, there is no relationship.

This is the simplest way I know to explain the concept that we can't change someone else but only ourselves. People's failure or even refusal to understand and apply this principle correctly is the root of countless broken hearts and wasted lives.

Here's what misunderstanding or misapplying the principle might sound like, in different situations. As a counselor, I am unfortunately all too familiar with such scenarios:

- "If I were a better wife, he wouldn't get so angry or be so violent with the children or me."
- "When we're married, all that will change."
- "I'll help him settle down and work hard—he'll have a family to support, after all."
- "If I love her enough, she'll come back to me."
- "She's the only one for me; I'll make her love me."
- "He can't just give up on this marriage; we've been together twenty years."
- "If I'm good enough, he'll follow me to church."
- "She can't ignore me if I work harder."

These comments and a thousand more like them miss the point. Individuals are free to choose where they are on the paper, or even if they want to be on the paper at all. The hardest part of this to understand, and possibly the most difficult to accept, is that even near-perfect

performance on your part does not guarantee any performance from your mate.

WHERE DID I GO WRONG?

How many times has a friend, a counselor, or a
bishop been asked, "What did I do wrong?" We're all
painfully aware that no one is perfect—friends, counselors, and bishops included. But, in many cases, the
practical answer to this heartfelt question is: Nothing.
Your mate just chooses not to be in this relationship any
longer. His or her dot is not on the page anymore. No
amount of wishing or crying or anger on your part can
change a decision that is not yours to make.

We've already discovered the real truth about a relationship—it takes two people who are committed to
make it work. But it takes only one person to divorce, to
end the relationship. Sometimes we need to be brave
enough to look at the ending of a relationship in the only
realistic way possible. If our spouse, the person we are
engaged to, or our significant other chooses to leave the
relationship, to take his or her dot off the page, it's that
person's right. We may hate it. It may hurt beyond reason. But it's still the person's right, and we can't change
that.

That doesn't mean all men are dot removers. It doesn't
mean no one wants to be a dot on our page, or that our
page is capable of attracting only "loser" dots. It may
mean someone made a bad choice and will someday be
sorry. But it was that person's choice, and whatever the

consequences of that choice are, they will and should belong to that person.

Am I saying that someone can never recognize this kind of mistake and decide to try rekindling a relationship? No. That person can decide to try again to be part of your life at any time. And you can decide at any time to let it happen.

What I am saying is, it's the right and responsibility of every individual to choose, and sometimes what someone else chooses hurts us.

But remember, sometimes there is value in adversity. Challenges, struggles, and disappointments provide us the opportunity to ask ourselves what we have learned from the experience. Often, these are the things that give us the motivation to look in the mirror and evaluate our performance.

I'm sorry to say that from time to time I've looked in the mirror only to find the person who made the poor choice staring me back in the face. If we are prepared to look honestly at our behavior, the ensuing self-discovery can be a valuable thing. If we have had a painful experience, we need to understand that it can be an important one as well, if we'll use it.

The Answer May Be in the Mirror

The importance of self-discovery is illustrated by the story of Jacob Thomas. Jake was a seasoned construction foreman in his mid-fifties who seemed stable and competent. He and his wife of more than twenty years were raising a happy and successful family. Jake knew his business and was a productive leader. He preached the importance of being prepared and accepting responsibility for one's actions.

Jake always told his workers, "The first place you need to look for the cause of a problem is in the mirror." He shared with several of us one day why the principle of self-evaluation was so important to him, and how he came to understand it.

He told of how, more than twenty-five years earlier, he had awakened in Las Vegas after one of the worst nights of his life. It was midday when he awoke. He remembered having fallen asleep early that morning in a rented tux. He'd been out "celebrating" the night before, alone, on a drinking binge. His divorce had become final the previous day, and he had determined that a party was in order. The last thing he remembered from the revelry of his freedom celebration was getting sick all over his beautiful tux. Evidence that his memory was accurate, along with a terrific hangover, greeted him as he awoke.

This was not a new experience for Jake. The most difficult part of the whole story was that the divorce that had ended his marriage the day before was not his first. It was his fifth. That morning, Jake was just a few days short of his twenty-eighth birthday. It was a morning that would change his life.

As he later recalled, he went to the mirror and beheld the tragedy that met his stare: soiled tux, scruffy beard, bloodshot eyes. As he beheld the mess in the mirror, a new thought came into Jake's mind: "Maybe it's me."

Unbelievable as it sounds, he had never before considered that his behavior and choices might have been part of the problem. He had blamed someone or something else through five failed marriages.

Actually, he'd blamed someone or something else for the troubles of his entire life up to that point. For more than twenty-seven years, some outside influence had "ruined his life." Someone or something always stood between him and happiness.

That morning, as he stood in that Las Vegas hotel room, Jake truly looked in the mirror for the first time. He saw a person even he wouldn't marry or live with. He saw a person he wouldn't trust in a partnership. He determined, correctly, that only he could change Jake, and he set about that very day to do just that.

As he told us this story, it seemed impossible that this model husband, father, and successful manager could have been the young five-time loser of so many years before. He decided that morning—when he faced the evidence before him for the first time—that the quality of person he was and the quality of life he chose to live was up to him. He was right, of course, and within a few months he met and later married his wife of twenty-plus years.

From that experience he learned a great truth, a truth he used in his life every day. When we encounter a problem or a roadblock, the first place to look for solutions is in the mirror. Sometimes the problem really does have roots elsewhere. But how we handle it—even when someone else is to blame—is entirely up to us.

FINDING OUT FOR YOURSELF

The Savior taught this principle of self-discovery in the parable of the prodigal son: "*And when he came to himself,* he said, How many hired servants of my father's have bread enough and to spare, and I perish with hunger! I will arise and go to my father, and will say unto him, Father, I have sinned against heaven, and before thee" (Luke 15:17–18).

That young man had to understand *his* role in the disaster that was his life. Only then could he see that the changes necessary to improve it were up to him. He had to come to himself.

Does this coming to self mean hitting rock bottom, as we often hear about in cases of substance abuse? Does it mean divorce or bankruptcy or financial ruin? Does it mean an affair and excommunication? No. We tell our children not to touch the stove because it is hot. Some of them wisely trust us and leave the stove alone without the need of being burned. Others suffer the consequences of a careless moment with a minor injury. This is where they learn the truth of our advice. Some willfully test and find out the truth about *hot* for themselves. Even the most rebellious and most injured of us generally learn, once burned.

That is why faithful obedience is not blind obedience.

It is generalized experience applied. When I have learned that a warning I got was a wise one, I have established the one who gave it as a credible source of information. Life has taught me to listen to those credible sources of warning. The prophet—as well as other trusted and tested teachers, leaders, and friends—can keep me from disaster, if I will pay attention. If I am humble enough to seek wise counsel and then listen when I get it, I need not learn from my pain alone. This is a good time to be reminded again of our advice to children seeking truth: search, ponder, and pray.

We can understand our responsibility to change ourselves, and our inability to change someone else, as we evaluate our lives, seek wise counsel, and choose the paths we will take. As painful as it is, each of us can change only one person: ourselves. We can help others, if they choose to let us. But whatever change needs to be made is theirs to make. We can be helped if we will allow it, but the change in our lives is up to us.

We can be a good or negative influence on those around us. We should strive to be as positive as possible. Positive or negative, however, how others respond to us is up to them—just as how we respond to others is up to us.

For all practical purposes, improved relationships are about change, growth, and education. Doing the work together is the most effective and productive way to change, grow, and learn. The best way to develop a relationship is together. One spouse understanding and growing positively is better than nothing, but the growth that occurs when both participants are guided by mutual commitment is most effective.

HOW LONG DO I KEEP TRYING?

How long should you strive with your mate? I wish I could give the right answer to that question. It is one I am asked over and over as a counselor, and I don't have the magic response. I can share one story, though, that has been enlightening for me.

One day in conversation over lunch, a friend asked me what I would do differently if I could change something in my life. Several things came to mind, mostly small and frivolous—a turn here or there that might have avoided some accident or broken bone, for example.

He had obviously done some thinking on the subject himself, and he said, "The biggest mistake I ever made was divorcing the kids' mom." I was aware that he had grown children and grandchildren; I was not aware that his current wife was not his first but his fourth. His three children were from his first marriage. He had become disenchanted with his first wife and left her for his much younger secretary. He said he had used a midlife crisis as his excuse, but, as he looked back now, he could see that the real reason was stupidity. By the time he came to his senses, he was in a very unhappy second marriage. He divorced a second time. Meanwhile, his first wife remarried, but he kept in contact with her and was a good father to their children in terms of interest and support.

He married a third time, and, despite his best efforts, that marriage also ended in divorce. He stayed single for almost twenty years before marrying his fourth wife, to whom he had been happily married for almost ten years by the time of our conversation. He said that with a little more patience and a lot more humility, he could have had a great marriage the first time. His greatest sorrow was in not having worked hard enough to keep what he had.

I don't know for sure how long we should keep trying or how much effort is enough. What I do know is what my friend taught me long ago. Marriage—in fact, anything of great value—can be hard work. The problem is like that of a gold-mining operation: After having made so much investment, you want to make sure you don't stop working just before you hit pay dirt.

That said, however, a warning about abuse is necessary. There is no excuse or rationalization to justify or compel any person to be part of any relationship that is unsafe for either spouse or child. Abuse of any kind is neither condoned nor tolerated by the Lord, his church, or the laws of the land. Anyone who suggests otherwise is wrong.

If your spouse is physically abusive, leave. Get yourself and your children to a safe place, and let your spouse work on his or her problem. Consult with priesthood leaders and law enforcement as required, and don't ever compromise your safety or that of your children.

Please take the matter of spouse and child abuse

seriously. The Lord's word is plain. No excuse exists for the abuse of spouse or child. We understand how the Lord feels about compulsion from reading in the Doctrine and Covenants:

> When we undertake to cover our sins, or to grat-ify our pride, our vain ambition, or to exercise control or dominion or compulsion upon the souls of the children of men, in any degree of unrighteousness, behold, the heavens withdraw themselves; the Spirit of the Lord is grieved; . . .
>
> No power or influence can or ought to be main-tained by virtue of the priesthood, only by persuasion, by long-suffering, by gentleness and meekness, and by love unfeigned;
>
> By kindness, and pure knowledge, which shall greatly enlarge the soul without hypocrisy, and with-out guile (D&C 121:37, 41–42).

Note the words "without hypocrisy, and without guile." These words reflect the condition of one's heart. The skills of a successful marriage are no good if not practiced by a sweet soul. A soul without hypocrisy and without guile is a soul prepared to learn. This is a person prepared to be enlarged by the kind of interaction the Lord describes, the interaction not of compulsion but of persuasion, long-suffering, gentleness, meekness, love unfeigned, kindness, and pure knowledge. It is interest-ing that in this powerful passage the Lord provides both the warning "not-to" and the hopeful "how-to" instruc-tion for relationships.

Understanding and Overcoming
Our Fear of Change

I remember taking my daughter to school on her first day of first grade. My experience told me she would be fine and that the experience was necessary for her education. Her point of view was very different. She could see no good reason to leave a perfectly good house with her toys and, more important, her mother to go among strangers. I went with her to her principal's office, and the three of us took courage and made the long walk to first grade together.

In her high school years, when she had some new obstacle to tackle, I often reminded her of that morning and offered to accompany her. I offered to go with her to her first cheerleading practice and even suggested I could find her old Scooby-Doo lunch box to take along for familiarity and comfort. She declined with vigor.

I'm not suggesting that all our trials are simple or unthreatening. What I know, however, is that we must not let the fear of change rob us of possibilities for the future.

The universe is in constant movement. Everything around us is in motion. The very molecules of each basic element are moving. The rivers, the planets, and every aspect of our lives are in a constant state of flux. Why, then, do we hold onto the myth of a status quo so tenaciously? We all experience change as a consequence of living. Only by accepting this reality and learning about it can we come to understand the process and potential of change in our lives.

After we have accepted that change is inevitable, we can see that managed, understood, or even directed change is better than chaos. Understanding and participating in the change process allows us the most possible impact. Life is complex, and the intricacies of our relationship to our environment and to each other make it impossible to control change completely. However, being aware of the process gives us the chance to move successfully in the direction of our choice.

There is a rule of thumb about change that sometimes renders us less than eager to be excited about the process, even if we desire its outcome. With apologies to the physicists, I offer the following: "There is no change in the universe without movement. No movement occurs without friction, and no friction occurs without heat."

We can assume, I think correctly, that no change takes place without some heat. We experience that heat in many different ways. Sometimes it is a slight discomfort, like wearing a new pair of shoes. We are usually willing to bear this brief discomfort because we know that shortly the feeling will pass. But often the heat of change is uncomfortable enough to keep us from being willing participants. Having the courage and knowledge to weigh the possible outcomes against the risk of taking some heat is what understanding and managing change is all about.

I love the thoughts of Theodore Roosevelt on the

rewards of participating fully in our own lives. As part of an address at the Sorbonne in Paris, France, on April 23, 1910, he said,

> It is not the critic who counts; not the man who points out how the strong man stumbles, or where the doer of deeds could have done them better. The credit belongs to the man who is actually in the arena, whose face is marred by dust and sweat and blood; who strives valiantly; who errs, and comes short again and again, because there is no effort without error and shortcoming; but who does actually strive to do the deeds; who knows the great enthusiasms, the great devotions; who spends himself in a worthy cause; who at the best knows in the end the triumph of high achievement, and who at the worst, if he fails, at least fails while daring greatly, so that his place shall never be with those cold and timid souls who know neither victory nor defeat.

The cost of change must be balanced not only against the possible rewards but also against the compound price we pay for choosing inaction.

- What damage is done by trying to hang on to an abusive spouse?
- If I don't get an education, will I ever be able to reach the employment objectives I desire?
- If we don't seek out the specialist, will we get the best advice on our son's condition?

A major roadblock to change is our inability or unwillingness to ask these kinds of questions.

Most often it is fear that keeps us from making and

acting on our evaluations of a need to change. Fear of the unknown, fear of pain, fear of failure—all are crippling, keeping us from moving forward.

William Shakespeare knew the crippling nature of this kind of fear. He wrote, "Our doubts are traitors and make us lose the good we oft might win by fearing to attempt" (*Measure for Measure*, act 1, scene 4).

WHERE DO I GO FROM HERE?

Dissatisfaction and discomfort prod us to recognize the need for change. If we are willing to take a closer look at our difficult situations, we will gain a better understanding of what is causing the discomfort. We can then evaluate the situations based on our education, understanding, and experience. If we need more information about what we are feeling or observing, this is the time to get it, from books, from the Internet, or from a professional counselor. A plan to eliminate problems or add more positive elements to our situation is the logical outcome of our observation and educated understanding.

It is during this evaluation process that fear most often raises its ugly head. But the antidote for fear is hope. If we can believe that the change we seek is possible for us—if we have that hope—fear can be overcome. Much too often the desire to change comes from desperation, not education or inspiration. You may have heard, for example, that a person with an addiction must "hit rock bottom" before he or she will change. When a person comes to a point when "anything is better than this," that person is at last willing to overcome fear long enough to try changing. At that point, a hope deep in the soul—that there must be a better way—is kindled. Even if the spark of hope is dim, the attempt at positive movement may get some positive results. And these results will further fan the fires of hope. Evidence of possibility brings courage, and with courage comes the energy to continue.

Understanding this cycle may help us recognize where we are in the change process on any given matter. That understanding may help us move forward. It may help us overcome our fear and resistance and better manage the inevitable. Hope can be habitual, and its fruit can be delicious.

Chapter 4

Decide to Be Married

Ninety percent of our problems can be solved if we will but make up our minds.
—*Franklin D. Richards*

We are responsible for attaching value to our feelings, possessions, and beliefs—in fact, our whole world. Only we have the power to determine what matters to us and how much. We set the prices for the things in our lives. We then add an exclamation point to that value with our actions.

I can only guess at the number of dollars and hours I have spent on my desire to enjoy the outdoors through fly-fishing. I have been in pursuit of the perfect stream, day, moment, trout, or other fly-rod experience for the better part of thirty years. I have traveled from the South

Pacific to the Bering Sea. If you want to get me in an animated conversation, just ask me about the stone-fly hatch on the Deschutes River in Oregon. I have great affection for my fly rods and reels. My guess is that many who read this would find my interest in the aquatic insects of the West more than a little amusing. The reason is not because of some fault in my character, although such has often been suggested in regard to my interest in the sublime art. The amusement would come from your lack of interest in what I believe to be important. This is, on the surface, a quaint and even silly example of how we place value on what matters to us. It is food for thought, however. Do we spend the appropriate amount of time on what really matters most in our lives? There is nothing wrong with my enjoying my chosen hobby. But what if the time and resources I spend on it take sustenance from what matters most? The most innocent-looking choices sometimes have the potential to cause great harm. I wonder if a spouse has ever asked which means more, fishing or the family? Of course that has been asked. Do any of these ring a bell?

- Is that car more important than our marriage?
- Aren't the clothes you already have enough?
- Why do we always have to visit relatives when we go on vacation? Don't you ever just want to be with our family?
- I know you love to play softball, but isn't there a single weekend this summer for us?

- Is the Young Women activity more important than our family?
- How can you spend so much time on church work when the house is such a mess?
- Is your golf game more important than our son?

There is a trap in such questions. They are asked in a way that implies an all-or-nothing relationship. We assume in our questions that we know for sure what the outcome of changing a certain behavior or revaluing an activity would have. For example, the question "How can you spend so much time on church work when the house is such a mess?" implies that if you did not spend this time doing church work, the time would be spent cleaning the house. What if the time you spend doing church work is what gives you the self-worth to keep going when life seems worthless? What if the time spent golfing is what keeps you from crumbling completely from the pressure of parenting or work? Fly-fishing, golfing, church callings, travel, craft projects—all the good things we do should contribute to our lives and the lives of our families. What we need to do is take a global look at what we are doing and how we prioritize the activities in our lives. Sometimes we are forced by our limited time and other resources to choose between good and good, not between good and evil. In spite of life's other demands, we need to be sure we are investing enough time, interest, and resources in our marriage.

Marriage is a choice of eternal consequences that binds you and your spouse in partnership with God.

Your marriage can be the source of everlasting reward, and it deserves time appropriate to that value.

Our recognition of how we value any possession is our willingness to protect and defend it, or how much time, money, energy, and interest we spend on it. We keep important papers in a safe, secure place. We make the time and commitment required to exercise constant vigilance over our bank accounts and other worldly possessions. We take the time to take care of what we value.

Exercise: What Do You Value?

List in a column on the left side of a blank sheet of paper eight things you value. The list below is not presented in any particular order of importance, and it is included only as food for thought. It should not bias your selections. Order your list by how important each of the items you include is to you.

- Wealth
- Health
- The gospel
- Employment
- Family
- Education
- Life
- Friends
- Home
- Citizenship
- Freedom

Now take a minute and on the right side of the same page write the percentage of your waking hours you spend on each. For example:

- Gospel   10%
- Employment   50%
- Family   20%
- Education   5%
- Health   5%

If you are like most people, the importance you feel about a given area may not be reflected in the time commitment it gets. This exercise can help you discuss what you might need to reorder in your life to best reflect what you know is important.

DO YOU WANT TO BE MARRIED?

Whenever I begin counseling with a new couple, several important things need to happen. There are the preliminary explanations and paperwork to be completed. Most people are sad and embarrassed even to be there. They often feel broken, incompetent, or overwhelmed, seeing counseling as a last-ditch effort that will let them say they have tried everything to save their marriage. Many people are wary of counselors and counseling. I don't blame them. Without some experience, counseling is like going to the dentist for the first time—it may be necessary, but that doesn't make it enjoyable. As with going to the dentist, however, many discover that their fear is unjustified. If and when the ache is relieved, they wonder why they waited so long. So I spend a minute to help them understand what to expect in the process. After the couple has begun to relax, and most do quite quickly, I ask them why they have come. Although specific explanations vary and commitment levels differ, most express a desire to be happily married. They each want to be valued and appreciated. I always begin with the same four questions:

1. Do you want to be married?
2. To him?
3. Do you want to be married?
4. To her?

If the answer to all four questions is yes, and most of the time it is, I announce that therapy is over. All that is left at this point is education and the effort of applying what we learn. The remainder of our time together will be spent learning how to do what we both want. It will be spent learning how to be married happily, forever. This may seem simple, but that does not always mean it is easy. What it does mean is with work, education, and understanding, a happy marriage is possible. We then begin the effort required to make it happen.

We must decide to live with a total commitment that reflects the worth and sacred nature of marriage. Living with this level of commitment makes abandonment of this priceless resource our last option. That level of commitment gives the active protection of and commitment to our marriage its appropriate priority.

Sometimes, in spite of all we've done or tried to do, our least-desirable outcome is the only viable option available to us. There are reasons why divorce may be inevitable, but they are extreme.

However, a vast number of divorces take place that don't need to. The activities and attitudes that led to them were avoidable, had both participants simply decided somewhere along the road—before the point of no return—that their marriage was a top priority.

HOW GOOD MARRIAGES DIE

The thing that kills many marriages is a lack of attention. Sadly, we often pay much more attention to how long our car goes between oil changes than to how long it's been since we spent meaningful time alone with our spouse. Ongoing marital maintenance is an outward manifestation of how much we value the marriage relationship. Attention is a manifestation of how much we care.

Commitment to marriage means playing no "what-if" games. It means avoiding the senseless and often destructive fantasy of:

- "What if I'd waited to marry or had met this other woman first?"
- "What if I wasn't married? I'd have the career of my dreams, be independent, travel, and have all the new clothes I wanted."
- "What if John and I had met first? He is so sensitive, he'd really appreciate me."

Do these thoughts or others like them sound familiar? If so, decide to be married and stop this harmful pattern. A wise aphorism comes to mind here: It is foolish to try to make pigs sing; the music is lousy, and it irritates the pig. We often fill our lives with reliving or reinventing past opportunities. Stop. The past is past, and trying to live there is both impossible and irritating. The present is where the possibility of creating a beautiful symphony exists. Don't waste your time thinking about the music you might have written. Instead, write now.

Being faithful to your marriage means just that. Make the conscious effort to be true. Don't just go through the motions because you're "stuck." Work every day to fulfill the contract you made. Make the effort required to have the relationship that both God and you intended when you started it.

No "What-If" Games

Commitment to marriage means setting aside once and for all the "what-if" games. Instead of spending the energy thinking about some "what might have been" scenario, take the time to explore the possibilities and opportunities to keep the relationship you already have vibrant and growing.

Instead of asking questions like these:

- What if I'd waited to marry and had met this woman first? (I'd be happy.)
- What if I wasn't married? (I'd have the career of my

dreams. I'd be independent. I'd travel. I'd have all the new clothes I want.)

• What if John and I had met first? (He is so sensitive, he'd really appreciate me. I'd be free to explore a relationship with him.)

You could be asking questions like these:

• How could I be happy without (the kids, my best friend, the great times we have shared and what lies ahead)?

• What if I wasn't married? (All I'd have is my job to look forward to. I'd be so alone when it comes to facing life's personal challenges. I'd have no one to share the fun of new places and thoughts with.)

• How can I better love my husband or wife?

• What can I do to help my spouse better understand me and what I need?

• How can I explore a relationship with him or her?

Take a minute to write down some thoughts about how you can do a better job of being completely committed to your marriage and your spouse. Some thought-provoking questions to start the creative juices might include:

• What can I do to contribute to making our life better?

• What should I be grateful for in our marriage?

• What can we do to make life more fun?

• What positive things can I do to show my appreciation for what we have together?

Exercise: What Are the Possibilities of Marriage?

Be possessed by the possibilities, driven by the opportunities, and overwhelmed daily by what you and your spouse can and will have, if you choose to. Answer the following questions, which are all just subsets to the question: What are you doing to take advantage of the possibilities your relationship offers?"

- Are you still actively engaged in having fun together?
- Do you schedule time to plan and shape your lives?
- Are you both looking for ways to recognize the contributions and accomplishments of the other?
- Do you delight in the skills and talents of your mate?
- Do you tell her?
- Do you tell him?
- Do you avoid being alone with the opposite sex as a matter of respect for your spouse?
- Do you listen when your spouse speaks to you?
- Do you share disappointments and concerns?
- Are you making the time to enjoy uninterruptible sexual intimacy?
- Are you sharing dreams and aspirations?
- Do you support each other's individual activities and interests?

This list could—and will—go ever onward. Note

that there's nothing listed there that you—given a moment's thought—might not have listed under the heading "How to Build a Relationship." The question is not always whether we know how to build a better marriage; many times it is whether we make the effort to bother.

Forget "what-ifs" and be married. Be committed. Choose to believe and have faith in the eternal contract of joy. The rewards are commensurate with the value you place upon your lives together.

THE DECISION IS YOURS

It's my honest belief that deciding to be married once and for all—and giving that commitment your heart and soul—is the single most important factor in the success of any marriage. Abraham Lincoln noted, "People are about as happy as they make up their minds to be." We can borrow that true principle and apply it here by saying, "People are about as happily married as they make up their minds to be."

Choose to be married. Choose to be fully engaged in making that marriage all it can be—a relationship lived with eternal covenants and consequences in mind. This is the prize, and it is worth the price!

PART 2

Perspective: Understanding the Possibilities

CHAPTER 5

You Always End Up Where You're Going

Alice: *Would you tell me, please, which way I ought to go from here?*
Cheshire Cat: *That depends a good deal on where you want to get to.*
—*Lewis Carroll*, Alice in Wonderland

$\mathcal{S}$ometimes the most important principles we discover in life are among the simplest. We intuitively recognize these concepts as correct. They are the things that make sense. Such key concepts can be so self-evident that we overlook them or just don't pay attention to them. One such profound and simple concept is this: We always end up where we're going.

HOW DID I GET HERE?

Let me illustrate with a story I remember being told by a visiting General Authority at a stake conference. I heard this story when I was a young man, and it changed

53

my life, demonstrating in an understandable way that the journeys we make take us exactly where we were headed the whole time:

"One day a high school friend entered my office. He had been a very popular young man in school and was not only a friend but had also been a member of my ward and priests quorum. We had grown up together.

"After we had exchanged the kind of small talk old friends do, he became serious. He described a life to me, his life, a life that had been less than he had hoped it would be. Then in a tearful plea for some kind of insight or understanding, he asked, 'How did I get here?'

"My answer came after a moment of prayerful consideration for my sweet friend. 'Bob,' I said, in the gentlest way I could, 'you ended up here because you were never headed anywhere else. You embarked on a road that led directly here. You chose every step of the way to do those things that would take you nowhere else.'"

That is the gist of the story as I remember it from my youth. I pondered it for a long time and understood it to be true. I realized that nearly all of us who are heading in the wrong direction know exactly where we are going. We even understand in our own hearts that it is the wrong direction. But for some reason we choose not to acknowledge this understanding, or we do see it and just hope it isn't so.

This is just as much the case with sin as it is with harmful or limiting decisions about our marriage.

The Road to Spokane

Here's another example. Downtown Seattle, Washington, is the West Coast origin for one of the nation's great freeways, Interstate 90. I-90 begins in the heart of the city and runs in a basically east-west direction between Seattle and Chicago, Illinois. That's a distance of approximately 2,066 miles.

Just as it begins, I-90 crosses another freeway— Interstate 5. I-5 is the major north-south artery running from the Canadian border in the north to the Mexican border in the south.

So, at the intersection of I-5 and I-90 in downtown Seattle, you have a simple choice to make: Which way do I go? Which road takes me to where I am headed?

Let's say you want to go to Spokane, in eastern Washington. (Let's assume that Spokane, for illustrative purposes, is the right place for us to end up. It represents happiness with a full and purposeful life). Spokane lies approximately 280 miles east via I-90.

Eugene, Oregon, on the other hand, lies 280 miles to the south via I-5. (Let's say Eugene is not the right place for us to end up, representing unhappiness and a directionless or empty life.)

If you want to reach Spokane, all you have to do is get on I-90, head east, and keep going.

Now, there are many ways to move in Spokane's direction. Some are more efficient than others. You could walk or drive a car. You could crawl or run or ride a bike.

Whatever means you choose, if you keep moving forward and stay on I-90, eventually you will get to Spokane.

There are all kinds of signs along the way indicating progress. What do the road signs or mileposts say? Have we crossed the Cascade Mountains yet? Have we gone through North Bend or Ellensburg? Are we getting closer? Is the speedometer registering some forward movement? Does the gas gauge say we're using fuel? Are the right scenes passing by our windows?

TAKING A WRONG TURN

My firm belief is that many of us, for whatever reason, find ourselves on the ramp that leads to I-5 southbound instead of I-90 heading east. We know we're heading in a direction other than the one we really want to go, but we decide that getting off our current ramp is a bit of a pain. We rationalize that the road we're getting on could take us to Spokane, eventually. *After all, we think, the on-ramps look pretty much the same, and I really want to go to Spokane. I'll just take a different route, and I'm sure I'll get there in the end.*

So we drive on and don't think much about it for a while. After all, it's a pleasant road, and we seem to be making good time. We don't even have to climb the Cascade Mountains on this road, so it seems a much easier way to get to where we're going.

Somewhere in the back of our minds, though, there's still the feeling that maybe we should turn back and take the road that leads directly to Spokane. The farther we go along the wrong road, the more difficult going back becomes. At least that is what we think. So we tell ourselves over and over that this is the road we want and that it will get us to Spokane.

We stop reading the signs that tell us we're headed the wrong direction. Or we read them and believe that they're all somehow wrong. After we've driven the expected 280 miles to Spokane, we look up and read a sign that says we're entering Eugene, Oregon.

We find ourselves out of gas, out of time, and in a place where we didn't intend to be. But it's the place we were headed for all along. The signs were accurate. That still, small voice in the very center of our hearts was right. We were on the wrong road and could end up nowhere else, without a course correction.

How sad to be out of gas, out of time, and in a place where we didn't want to be.

So What's to Be Learned?

There are several valuable lessons to be learned from what that visiting General Authority taught so many years ago. First, and perhaps most valuable, is that there is a road to take us directly where we want to go. Whether we call it I-90, the strait and narrow path, the iron rod, or an obedient life doesn't matter. What matters is that the way to find eternal joy and peace, to live with our Father and heavenly family again, is available to each of us. We need to choose the right road and endure. It doesn't matter what our relative speed is; if we keep going on that road, we will all get there.

Another lesson to be learned is that as soon as we realize we're going the wrong way, we can go back and start again. Henry Ford said, "Failure is just the opportunity to begin again more intelligently." We can do just that, any time we choose. We need to read the signs and pay attention to our feelings and the still, small whisperings of our hearts. We innately know what road is right. It may not be the easiest or the most fun, but we know in our hearts where the road we are on is headed. If that road is not going where we hoped or intended, we must stop and begin the journey again—more intelligently this time.

How to Get Started Again

Here's the good news for the traveler who finds himself or herself on the wrong road. The Savior has made a special arrangement for each of us, if we're wise enough to take advantage of it. The arrangement is repentance. When we find ourselves down the wrong road, no matter how far, all we have to do is ask the Lord for a new start. He will take us back to the beginning of the road, fill our tanks, tune our engines, give us a map, and start us again in the right direction.

We may have lost some time. But what's true in the beginning is true still. If we get on the proper road and endure (keep going), we will end up where He and we wanted and intended us to be.

The Gift of Perspective

Sometimes the best way to stay on the road is to get a better look at the whole map. Keeping an eternal perspective can really change how we deal with the stretch of life's highway we're currently navigating. But how easily we seem to forget what counts! A friend suggested to me that this is just a matter of space. Our conscious mind has only so much room. When a spiritual experience or intense emotional moment has just occurred, it seems so important that we feel we'll never lose its impact. But as life goes on, our mind of necessity stores that experience in a safe place. It does that to free up the short-term brainpower needed to handle the demands of the present.

This theory works for me. It helps me see that keeping an eternal perspective is my responsibility. It requires me to keep certain valuable thoughts, feelings, and experiences alive and vibrant in my mind. Keeping order allows those stored magic moments to be retrieved. I often need to remind myself, or be reminded, of the things that matter most.

The Things That Matter Most

The wording of the sacrament prayers is no accident. He who understands us completely has infinite perspective, knows our needs, and shows us the way. He shows us how to keep those things that should mean the most to us fresh and clear in our minds and hearts. Consider the model He gives us concerning our responsibility to keep our covenants fresh in our minds in the sacrament prayers:

> . . . that they may eat *in remembrance* . . . and *always remember him* . . . that they may always have his Spirit to be with them (D&C 20:77).
> . . . that they may do it *in remembrance* . . . that they do *always remember him,* that they may have his Spirit to be with them (D&C 20:79).

If I want to keep an eternal perspective about my marriage, it's my responsibility to remind myself often why I love my wife so much. I must never forget why I married her and made an eternal promise to stay married to her, to love, honor, and cherish her.

It's my opportunity to often remind both of us how wonderful she is, and how many wonderful things there are about her. She's very bright, she has a wonderful sense of humor, and she is beautiful and kind. She's honest and dependable. Her smile shames the sunrise, and she's a remarkable friend. I like her as much as I love her. She is the kind of person I wish I were and I am trying to become. It's also my chance to remind myself that I'm capable of being worthy of her if I keep that objective active and living in my heart and mind.

What I Must Never Forget

I remember a dark night, one of the darkest of my life, about twenty-five years ago in a little hospital in New Mexico. We had been married more than a year, and we had a new daughter just three weeks old.

There were complications after the birth, and my wife, Lois, lay in bed in the small, dark hospital room, suffering from a peritoneal infection that had her at the very doors of death. She was delirious with fever, whimpering in her fitful sleep. I will never forget that sound—it tore my heart out.

But she'd received a blessing, and the doctor was hopeful. He said if she lived through the night and the fever had not been too damaging, she might recover fully.

I won't go into the conversation I had with my Father in Heaven by her bedside on that cold and lonely February night, but I'll tell you one thing: I knelt in earnest prayer, and as I poured out my heart there was no doubt in my mind how valuable my wife was. There was not a single second of that horrible experience in which I did not know just how important my marriage covenant and my sweet young wife were to me.

Have I been a perfect husband since the blessing of her recovery? Not even close. Nobody is perfect, and so neither is my performance.

But I've reviewed that night in New Mexico many times in my heart. And I've remembered my promises to my Father in Heaven and my commitment to my wife. That moment (and others)—when reviewed with the Spirit—have brought me the recommitment and motivation of perspective. When I'm prideful or just foolish and let things matter that don't, it's been helpful to remember the woman I'm married to, and why I married her. It also reminds me of whom she married and what she has the right to expect from me.

That kind of perspective has the power to change our hearts and motivate us to improve. I have a favorite scripture that I recall when I need to make an adjustment in my eternal perspective. It helps me understand that just because we've had a wonderful or significant experience, that doesn't mean we'll automatically recall it to full advantage in our lives. It does remind me, though, that it's possible with some effort to do so. With a little concentration, I can recall not just the memory but also the life-changing feelings that accompanied the experience. In the following excerpt from Alma we are reminded of the power of such remembering: "If ye have experienced a change of heart, and if ye have felt to sing the song of redeeming love, I would ask, can ye feel so now? Have ye walked, keeping yourselves blameless before God? Could ye say, if ye were called to die at this time, within yourselves, that ye have been sufficiently humble?" (Alma 5:26–27).

Clearly what Alma is referring to is not simple recall but bringing to bear the complete emotional experience. It's inviting the spirit of the experience once more to teach us truth, to bring us the light of perspective. We can then use that light to show us the way to get our lives back on track and be moved to constructive action.

The prophet Moroni recognized the need for that light in our lives and made a promise in the Book of Mormon about how we could get it. He endorses the prayerful and contemplative request for the teaching spirit of the Holy Ghost to confirm the value of what we've received. He says, in Moroni 10:5, "By the power of the Holy Ghost ye may know the truth of all things."

I am often asked in counseling if I am not just kidding myself and my client. Don't I realize that there is not really much to be grateful for with Frank or Barb? I respond by saying that it doesn't hurt to take another look. Perhaps the image would look more promising from another perspective.

THE LIAHONA THAT IS MARRIAGE

Having and being a companion in the tough tests we face in our lives can be an advantage. I have always found a particular passage of scripture interesting as it relates to the positive possibilities of a supportive marriage. The scripture speaks of the Liahona or director given to Lehi and his family as a guide to show them the way to go in the wilderness. This director worked by faith. The thing I find so interesting is the design of this revelatory gift as described by the prophet Nephi. He describes two spindles or pointers in the ball as the means of confirming the faith of the people: "I, Nephi, beheld the pointers which were in the ball, that they did work according to the faith and diligence and heed which we did give unto them" (1 Nephi 16:28).

We don't really know how the Liahona worked, but one possibility is that if Lehi and his family were faithful and diligent, the spindles would both point in the same direction, indicating the way the family should go. If the family was not faithful and diligent, however, perhaps each pointer showed a different direction, representing confusion and disagreement.

There's no way to know for sure that the Lord designed the Liahona in this way. Nevertheless, this description serves well as a model for the power of an effective marriage partnership. If we are both working faithfully under the influence of the Spirit, we can confirm each other's thoughts and feelings. We can also confirm the presence of the Spirit of the Lord in our lives.

This would provide support in the wilderness that is our current earthly condition. How many times in our lives would it be valuable to have a partner to validate or support our feelings or decisions about something? Would it be a valuable resource to have—at our disposal—a sounding board that worked by faith and could verify that the direction we've chosen is the right way to go?

IF HE GUIDES US, HE IS AWARE OF US

The miracle of the Liahona is that it serves to confirm not only the direction to go but also the love and support of God as well. The presence of His Spirit confirms the participation of our Father in Heaven in our lives. It lets us know He is interested in us, loves us, and is available to us. One of the most remarkable things about our loving, caring Father is His availability. I find no end of joy in the irony that I, the person who can't even get the cable installer to call me back, can have a personal interview with the most powerful Being in the universe whenever I choose. There is no time limit, no appointment to make, and no limit to His interest in me. He is there and will confirm His love, support, and attention through the influence of the Holy Ghost.

So it is when partners seek the Spirit in guiding their decisions. The trusting confirmation of our eternal companion offers support, care, and confidence as we respond to the challenges offered by life. Consulting about difficult decisions binds us together, builds trust and communication, and helps us both feel involved, valued, and needed.

God knows us. He knows who and how we are. He knows what we need and what will help us survive this world, with all its spiritual challenges and tests. He planned for a celestial mate to be one of our resources; a faithful, supporting, and loving companion; a compass to help us find our way home.

CHAPTER 6

Men and Women Are Different

Trying to do well and trying to beat others are two different things. Excellence and victory are conceptually distinct and are experienced differently.

—*Alfie Kohn*

$\mathcal{T}$here must have been something about the person you married that drew or draws you to him or her. Part of what draws us and holds us together is gender.

DIFFICULTY OR CELEBRATION?

Seeing and experiencing the difference between the sexes as either problematic or nonexistent misses one of marriage's central (and possibly most hopeful) themes: The differences between us should be celebrated! These differences are part of what give the combined talents, propensities, abilities, and experiences of our relationship a broader range of possibilities.

Gender is one of those things that is significant to most of us. But it's a difficult subject to get a handle on because we're at the same time so serious and so silly about it. We're so intuitive and yet so incredibly stupid about it.

If you are like me, you can still remember parts of your first-grade learning experience. One of the things I remember is basic bathroom-request etiquette. We learned how and when to raise our hand and where to go. Chief on the "where to go" list was the mantra of elementary gender direction: boys with boys and girls with girls. Right then and there Mrs. Stotaher drew the first line in the sand I remember with regard to sorting by gender. Given that potty humor was in vogue in the first grade, we could almost always get a laugh simply by repeating the phrase "Boys with boys and girls with girls." We accepted intuitively this basic gender difference. Later in life, the concept of how gender chemistry contributes to our emotional and physical state is often never even considered. But the fact that at a very basic level boys and girls are different should invite us to at least consider whether that variable comes into play as we interact. It may or may not, but ignoring it makes no sense.

Many social norms and taboos involve gender roles. The fact that many of these expectations were developed (or began to be developed) at a young age can make them deeply imbedded, and they vary by culture, family, and individual. The people who taught us and raised us seemed to know exactly how we should act. There was, for the most part, no shortage of advice about how we should behave. Much of this was based on gender. We're defined in part by which roles we accepted for ourselves from the vast smorgasbord of those offered to us as we grew. Of equal importance are the roles we ascribe to others, based on our learned assumptions about gender. These assumptions can affect our relationships dramatically.

Depending on our backgrounds, we may have been taught and accepted gender-based assumptions without taking time to think about their validity and where they came from. We may continue to make these assumptions without challenging whether they make sense now.

Exercise: Gender Roles and Expectations

The following comments have been made as factual assertions in seminars and counseling sessions in the past. Are they true? This list is intended to provide material for you to begin examining your thoughts about gender roles and expectations. Add your own thoughts and beliefs. This would be an excellent outline to begin a discussion of gender with your spouse. Such a discussion should be less about right and wrong than about exploring what you believe about gender.

- Men earn the money.
- Women don't like football.
- Men don't cry.
- Women weep at the drop of a hat.
- A mother's role is to discipline the children.
- A father's role is to discipline the children.
- Men are aggressive and violent.
- Women are passive and nonviolent.
- Women who work outside the home are bad mothers.
- Fathers and sons go hunting.
- Women do handwork.

Like many of our biases, gender-related thinking is often expressed in absolutes. Use the list below as a tool to discover your gender biases. Complete the sentences below. Don't think about them; just finish them with the first thing that comes to mind. If nothing else, this is great fun to do with a group of friends. Again, this is less about right and wrong than it is about exploring what you believe. The discussion material here may be some fun as well.

- Men always . . .
- Men should . . .
- Men never . . .
- Why can't men . . .
- If only men could or would . . .
- Women always . . .
- Women should . . .
- Women never . . .
- Why can't women . . .
- If only women could or would . . .

READING ABOUT OURSELVES

A best-selling book, *Men Are from Mars, Women Are from Venus,* went to great lengths to tell us that men and women are different. For providing this vital information, the author had a best-seller and apparently did a lot of good.

I mention the book not to minimize the good it may have done but rather to ask a question: Shouldn't the fact that men and women are different have been blatantly obvious?

Yet many things about us are the same! Our defining and central role as children of our Heavenly Father is the same. Our basic humanity is very much the same. Our willingness to interact and our need to be involved in community, though perhaps expressed differently by gender, are basic to our humanity.

However, there are potentially major gender differences physically, emotionally, socially, and spiritually. For our purposes here, why these gender differences occur doesn't matter. The fact that they exist—and that these differences affect how we relate to each other—is the real point.

The writer of *Men Are from Mars, Women Are from Venus* was successful not only because he told us that we were different but also because he suggested what those differences were and how they affected us. These differences can apparently be used to predict how males and females will behave and interact. Maybe that's true, but what if you're married to that one-in-a-hundred individual who doesn't behave the way the book predicts? We must communicate as partners to discover our differences, not assume we know what they are based on gender alone.

SHOULD WE CARE ABOUT DIFFERENCES?

There's value in understanding that differences in gender exist. By understanding, we're forewarned of potential areas of conflict and misunderstanding. This information should help us move from the dangerous assumption that you're like me, to the understanding that we need to confirm, by communicating, what we think we know about you and me, and how we think and act.

Sir Francis Bacon is attributed with the Latin epigram "Nam et ipsa scientia potestas est" (Knowledge is power). Knowing that we're different alerts us to the potential danger of assuming sameness. As we'll discuss later in detail, it also alerts us to the vast positive potential of the complementary partnership between man and wife.

If we look at all women and all men and compare them in almost any physical, emotional, intellectual, or social category, there are many overlapping tendencies on every variable. Not only are we different because of our gender, but we also differ as individuals within and between our gender groups. In our individual desires, needs, and wants, we all have certain predispositions— not just gender predispositions but individual differences based on choice, family background, and almost as many other variables as one might list.

COMPLEMENTARITY AND COMPETITION

We are currently struggling in our culture with an insidious philosophy that can really damage marriages. This philosophy places the men and women who are trying to build a healthy partnership in a real hole, perhaps without their even knowing it.

I'm reminded of a saying attributed to Abraham Lincoln: "The first thing you should do when you realize you're in a hole is stop digging." Let's hope in this case that forewarned is forearmed, and that we can get out of this trap or avoid it.

The philosophy I'm referring to is the widely held notion that men and women are somehow inevitably in competition. It's not a competition for any particular reward or honor I'm aware of. It's a basic belief that by virtue of our gender alone we're in some adversarial great race for a single (unknown) prize—a prize, by the way, that only one person out of every couple can win.

The concept that men and women are different is a notion that's not only inherently sensible to us but a biological fact. If we are different, and we are, the next logical question in the argument for gender competition seems to be, Which of us is better? The implication is that such a judgment is necessary and that we're each compelled to make it.

I don't believe that such a judgment is even possible.

It brings to mind other great questions. Must these be answered if we're to come to the truth? Which is more beautiful, sunrise or sunset? Is apple pie or chocolate cream the best? Who is the opposite sex, you or me?

Do these questions cause the morning and evening to rage against each other, or great pie wars to erupt? Do they even make sense to ask?

Absolutely not. We simply accept sunrise and sunset as beautiful expressions of God's handiwork. Different kinds of pie offer us a chance to appreciate that freedom of choice sometimes means a decision between good and good. They're merely different.

That's the miracle of it. The beauty of diversity is evident in sunrise and sunset. It's there in the choice between apple and chocolate cream pies. It's there in comparing men and women, too.

That difference is not competitive but complementary. We don't have to choose one or the other; we can appreciate both. Appreciating one doesn't diminish the other.

In business, we easily accept the idea of a partnership where each member brings unique and valuable talents and skills to the arrangement. In fact, we embrace it.

Within companies, we depend on various departments—marketing, accounting, shipping—to make everything work. Each department performs tasks necessary for the organization to be successful.

In football, each person plays a position on the team. In a play or a symphony, we recognize without question that every person has a part. Without each individual part, something would be lost.

In gymnastics, each individual has specialties that contribute to the team score. Personal contributions can be recognized and still be helpful to the team.

Support Can Bring Success

The concept of a complementary marriage partnership based on love and trust between two healthy, contributing individuals is the most divinely sensible arrangement for success in life that I can imagine. Such a partnership, to be successful, requires the broadest set of skills, talents, and gifts of any partnership I can think of.

The simple fact that we're not always at our best—physically, mentally, or spiritually—means that we need another trusted ally to provide a helping hand on occasion. Loving reciprocity creates our opportunity to contribute. As Paul put it, "Neither is the man without the woman, neither the woman without the man, in the Lord. For as the woman is of the man, even so is the man also by the woman; but all things of God" (1 Corinthians 11:11–12).

Understanding our individual differences is a first step, and it is a big one. The next challenge may be even more arduous. We must begin the task of coming to understand how we came to be what we are.

CHAPTER 7

Your Family, My Family, Our Family

Experience is not what happens to a man. It is what
a man does with what happens to him.
—Aldous Huxley

We now have the opportunity to better understand the dynamics of creating a new family. When we got married, we altered two extended family systems and created another. That creative process opens the doors for further adventure, challenge, and fun.

Three family systems are involved when a new family is created by marriage: the bride's family of origin, the groom's family of origin, and the new family they create by marrying. To better understand the complexities of associating these different family entities, we need to identify whom we're talking about and what types of families we belong to. Two kinds of families need to be described.

First is the family into which we are born. It's identified as our *family of origin.* It does not matter what structure that family takes. It can even change its structure over time as its members redistribute themselves. For example, if your parents divorce and one or both remarry, you have two separate families of origin. Even though step-parents, step-siblings, and step-grandparents are adopted, not biological, members of the original family group, they may play a significant role in how your extended families relate. Their impact depends on how long they've been part of the family and how close you've become to them.

The second family is your *family of procreation.* This is you, your spouse, and your children, if you have children. This is your immediate family as a married adult. This is the family system that, if you procreate or adopt, your children will call their family of origin.

DIFFERENT PERSPECTIVES

It's in our families of origin that most of us learn how to live. We learn what's important or valuable, what roles we play and how to play them.

Here's the way the plan for being a family is intended to work. Our parents model and teach what they believe is valuable. We learn how to be the parents, citizens, and people they hope we will be. Because our parents are not perfect (just like us), the plan provides for us to evaluate their model and teachings. We then improve on them where we can so our model and teachings will be better for our children. In turn, they are encouraged to do the same.

In our families of procreation, we get the chance to put our new, improved spousal and parental model to work. As parents, this is our chance to build a new and improved family. In order to do this we must recognize that ours is a new independent family and knowingly set out to make it the best we can. That's the challenge of building a new family. It's the opportunity that marriage gives, the chance to make the world in general and our world in particular a better and more peaceful place. We can, by our choices, make the changes in our families of procreation that we'd like to have seen in our families of origin.

PERSONAL DIFFERENCES

As spouses, we're different not only in gender, as we've discussed, but also in how we were raised. Different people taught us how to be a person. We were taught in different social, emotional, environmental, and even cultural settings.

One useful model some counseling professionals use for looking at families is "family systems." A family system includes extended family and in many cases even close friends or neighbors if they played a significant role. The assertion here is that it's meaningful and important to look at individuals in the context of families. We need to look at people as part of a group, a family system, including families of origin and procreation. We need to recognize the impact of our extended families as well as our family history and traditions.

A FINE ART MODEL

Remember mobiles, those art objects invented by sculptor Alexander Calder? Mobiles are conglomerates of items (often very colorful) hung from a single point, usually by a wire or string. They're designed to hold everything hung from them in perfect balance. They are often very complex and can move about their point of suspension subtly or dramatically, depending on the forces acting on them.

That's how family systems are. They're all attached, sometimes in complex ways. And they try to balance. Because they're all connected, when movement or change occurs in one place, often somebody in another part of the family moves in response in order to try to keep that balance. Extended family systems are interrelated and have most likely, over time, come to some kind of equilibrium. The job of extended families seems to be to adjust all the individual parts, attempting to keep everything in balance.

My dad was an alcoholic most of the time I was growing up. (He quit drinking late in life, enjoying the peace and blessings of the gospel, and finally allowed himself to experience the love the Savior always had for him.) I was afraid for the most part to invite anybody to our house. In my growing up years I never knew what to expect at home. When you ventured into our house, it was like walking into a minefield. Some days you could go in and Dad was just fine. Other days, he wouldn't be, and emotional explosions could ensue. There was no way to know which situation you would encounter until you walked through that door.

On the one hand, it taught me to be cautious when trusting or depending on people or situations. On the other, it prepared me to be a successful salesperson and later an effective counselor and manager. I'm always more comfortable if I know how everyone else is feeling—evaluating the minefield, so to speak.

It's my experience that a lot of nurses, doctors, counselors, and other helping professionals come from alcoholic families where the empathetic helping model is one they understand well: "My feelings and needs don't matter right now; let's talk about your feelings and needs." Such an attitude can be really effective if you're a counselor. Would anyone want a counselor who started out with his clients by saying, "Shut up, stupid! Let me tell you how I feel."

So in this case, a family situation I might have initially construed as a tough thing was a blessing in the long term. The adaptive style I developed illustrates how we adjust to create balance in our families.

MARRIAGE CHANGES THE BALANCE

When people get married, a new family is created. Family A (the husband's family of origin) and family B (the wife's family of origin) each send a member to this new family.

And guess what? This new family is not simply an amalgam, family A/B. Instead it's family C, a brand new family—a new entity, a new mobile that seeks to balance its parts in a meaningful and independent way.

Often, at first, family C plays such an active part in families A and B that those families don't recognize the new entity as separate or distinct. They exert all kinds of pressure on family C to make it balance within their existing systems.

However, as time passes and the new family asserts its independence (if family C is wise enough to do so), families A and B readjust and balance themselves, with family C as an appropriate associated appendage. This can be a difficult and painful process. It can go on for years and perhaps never really happen if not actively managed.

MY VERSION OF THE CHRISTMAS STORY

When I got married, I thought there were two kinds of people in the world: those who opened their presents on Christmas morning, and Communists. I'm sure you are wise enough to recognize this position as a bit exaggerated. But that's how I felt, expressed tongue in cheek.

My wife's mother worked all night at Western Union and didn't get home until just after eight in the morning. She thought it was cruel to make Lois and her seven siblings wait until that late on Christmas morning to open their presents. In response to their particular situation, Lois's family chose to open presents on Christmas Eve.

After Lois and I got married, at my first Christmas Eve family party at Lois's mom's house, I commented that I could hardly wait until the next morning to see what Santa had for us. Her family said, "Oh, you don't have to wait. We're opening the presents tonight."

Wrong! Anyone who doesn't have the personal integrity to leave those presents wrapped until morning should be punished!

I felt strongly about this, as you can tell. Those feelings were very intense for me. The reason is, family rituals and traditions are often filled with powerful and well-defined emotions, processes, roles, and expectations.

Exercise: How Did You Do Things?

In an exercise or as a discussion, explore how the events in the following list were experienced by you or your spouse in the past. Note the similarities and differences, and what changes you'd like to consider, making notes as you discuss them. Add other rituals, traditions, and events to consider. As you negotiate your way through the discussion, remember that this process is sometimes a difficult and emotional one. The objective is to be aware of the potential for damage or joy and to manage it accordingly. Learn what's best for your family and remember to keep in mind that what matters most is not the process but the people.

Ask each other, "How have you experienced the following occasions?"

- Family reunions
- Births (of your children, extended family, brothers and sisters, roommates)
- Marriages (of extended family, brothers and sisters, roommates)
- Funerals
- Family vacations (Who with? When? Where? How often?)
- Holidays and other significant family moments, such as baptisms.

Such events are typical occasions for family rituals. Christmas is a prime example. The following are questions you can discuss about how Christmas should be celebrated:

- Whose house do you go to for each holiday?
- What do you cook?
- Who hangs the lights?
- When do you put up the tree?
- What kind of tree?
- Do you read the Christmas story?
- Who reads it?
- When?

The point is, when families A and B get together in a new marriage, we don't automatically have a map for building family C. It takes some conscious choices.

This would also make a good discussion. Include what you've both noticed in your two families of origin and other families you've observed. Remember: This is not, for the most part, a question of right or wrong but one of preference and tradition.

Discuss:

- Similarities.
- Differences.
- Changes you'd like to consider.

Over time, watch your parents, your siblings as they marry, and your own behaviors as in-laws. Sometimes family A or B or both don't want the new family to become family C. Why?

Because:

- "I know the in-laws and they stink."
- "They'll ruin my grandchildren."
- "Family A (our family) is the best family, and family B is a bad family. That's what family B stands for— bad."
- "If you don't stay as family A, you become family C, the creepy family."
- "You shouldn't want to spend time with family B. Those people don't even open their presents on Christmas morning! How could you want to spend time with such heathens?"

No Laughing Matter

At arm's length, sentiments like those are funny. But just wait until your son calls and says, "As you know, Mom, we were planning to come for Christmas this year. But I got cholera, so we're going to my wife's family for Christmas. They've all had cholera." Cholera or not, that's your child, choosing to go somewhere else!

Although potentially damaging, these examples we reviewed are pretty tame illustrations of family rules, rituals, and expectations, and how they affect the individuals involved. But they show that real differences exist between families—differences that pose potential problems. Sometimes we have trouble understanding each other. It might even be hard to understand what we were taught in our own homes. We find ourselves asking these questions about what we were taught:

- Is it right or not?
- Does it create a problem?
- Why was I taught that?
- Who said that, and why?
- Does that make sense for me?
- Where did that come from?

Keep in mind that what works in one family system or culture might not work in another. Maybe there was once a useful purpose for a given standard, process, or teaching that has, over time, become unnecessary or ineffective. Nevertheless, it has been ritualized as a part of our family tradition. It has become our standard, ineffective or not.

DIFFERENCES ARE INEVITABLE

To be effective partners, we must understand our family systems and the other components of our backgrounds that make us different from each other.

That doesn't mean that Lois was right or I was right about when to open Christmas presents. It does mean that we saw the situation differently, for reasons that made sense to each of us. The critical thing to remember is that differences are inevitable. But these inevitable differences can be investigated and discussed. We can decide how to handle them in the future. We can decide what works best for us.

What happens when roles or expectations developed in our families of origin have a negative impact on how we feel about others or ourselves? Some family myths or expectations can be damaging to you or someone you love. Many of these negative messages may be well-intentioned in the beginning but somehow leave the wrong result.

Some are easy to spot. Others may rise up to bite you, even after years of marriage. These harder-to-see messages are all those roles, rules, lies, and myths that exist perhaps without our even knowing they're there. But they're real, and they can become stumbling blocks.

Such things may go unchallenged for years. If they don't come into direct conflict with overpowering evidence that they're false, or become directly harmful or painful, we don't even acknowledge they exist. Perhaps we just don't know they're there, or maybe we just choose not to acknowledge them. To find these hidden time-bomb teachings that may be ticking behind the scenes, look for traditional family statements or beliefs that are always stated in the absolute. Some examples:

- Everyone opens Christmas presents on Christmas morning.
- Husbands who love their wives don't play basketball on weeknights, send flowers often, and call from work twice every day.
- To ask for help is failure.
- Women who work are bad mothers.
- Anybody who gets sick is trying to avoid something.
- Discussing money just causes fights.
- Reading is a way to ignore me.
- The house must be completely clean before anything else can be done.
- The wife is responsible for paying the bills.
- The husband is responsible for paying the bills.
- You must work as many hours as you can to succeed.
- All the men in this family have bad tempers.

You may recognize some of these. Or maybe you recall other similar ideas that are specific to your own family. Their hallmark is that they're statements of absolute belief, specific to us. Often they're the scripts by which we live.

Playing Our Parts

The roles assigned to us in the play of life are generally handed out in our youth by people older and seemingly wiser than we are. Early in our lives, we've neither the power nor the experience to question them effectively.

Thankfully, much of the time these directors of our life roles are kind and wise, recognizing our talents and potential. However, far too often people who (for whatever reasons) are unkind, self-serving, threatened, or just not very aware or bright are in a position to place labels on us.

Some of the roles in the following lists may sound familiar. One way to sniff out these potentially damaging absolutes in our lives is to use the fill-in-the-blank method.

Exercise: What's My Role?

Have you ever heard or said:

- He/she is the _____ one in the family.
- She/he always (or never or won't or can't or shouldn't) _____.

By filling in the blanks with the first words that come to mind, we can often identify the role assignments or expectations for ourselves or others that are familiar from our past.

Give it a try. Exchange the words in parentheses below with the italicized word or phrase to create different negative or positive examples. Feel free to add others that sound familiar to you. Record your answers on a piece of paper as you discover what your expectations have been of your various roles.

- He's the *lazy* one. (smart/stupid/quiet/funny/happy/dishonest)
- She's the *stupid* one in the family. (smart/lazy/quiet/slow/funny/happy/dishonest)
- She's the *wild* one in the ward. (Molly Mormon/ spiritual/rebellious/bossy/dull)
- He's the *smart* one in the class. (best/worst/brightest/silliest/with the most potential)
- She's always *late.* (angry/happy/studying/talking/asking questions/showing off)
- He never *gets it right.* (quits/learns anything/forgets anything/understands anything/makes trouble)

Sometimes role assignments or behavioral expectations are stated as a question. They're almost always stated in absolute terms as well, using words like never, always, or ever. For example:

- "Why can't you ever . . . ?"
- "Why must you always . . . ?"
- "Why can't you just _____?" (shut up/learn/listen/stop pushing/grow up/do what I tell you)

WHO GETS THE BLAME?

This book is not about placing blame or accusing parents, siblings, or extended family members of not being perfect. Nor is it about developing a master list of which rules, expectations, or roles work or don't work.

I'm in no position to decide why you were taught what you were, or why you chose to believe what you did—just as I can't know why you rejected other things people were trying to teach you. Certainly no one's suggesting some global parental conspiracy to make children crazy or create ineffective adults.

The reality is, we're all taught in one way or another about life, and some of those lessons are not on the mark. Some of what you were taught will be problematic for your spouse and your marriage. Almost surely, elements of what you were taught or learned will be in conflict with what your spouse was taught or learned. It is valuable to be aware of this and review what you believe together.

You need to decide what works for you two—what new or different things you'll choose to try—as you refine your marriage relationship and bring your family of procreation into peaceful balance.

Proactive creation of a positive family C environment means spending less time on the whys of the past and more time on the whats of the future. When a troublesome rule, role, myth, or lie is discovered, evaluate it, learn from it, and then discard it and move on. Don't waste time with blame or bile. The question is, What do we replace it with that works for us? Setting positive expectations for our marriage exposes these hidden obstacles and sets the stage for understanding and communication.

PART 3

Skills: Making the Possible Real

CHAPTER 8

Marriage Therapy—Try This at Home!

*Far and away the best prize that life offers is the chance
to work hard at work worth doing.*
—*Theodore Roosevelt*

Healing is a personal process. In his book *Simply Sane,*
Dr. Gerald May describes healing as a natural process
between God and the person being healed. The physician's role in physical healing and the clinician's or counselor's role in mental or relational health is to provide the
conditions where natural healing occurs most easily.

To quote Dr. May, "Whatever the illness or injury, the
role of the physician is relegated to three primary
activities:

"1. To bring the diseased or injured part back to a
more natural state.

"2. To cleanse and purify.

"3. To provide rest."

This is the same process that defines professional marriage therapy. It's all about providing the conditions to facilitate growth and healing. The counseling provided by a competent professional is just one of many tools couples can use to improve their relationship. But remember that a therapist, no matter how capable or talented, can't heal or grow for you.

In that same vein, supplying practical information and helping you build an environment that will strengthen your marriage is one of the important roles this book can play. Whether you see a therapist or find help here or elsewhere, the ongoing healing and development of your marriage belongs to you and your spouse. That's the essence of marriage therapy. The content and application of that therapy is yours.

You may ask, "How can we do marital therapy on ourselves? We're not trained professionals." The sage advice of daredevils and carnival performers, "Do not try this at home," rings in our ears. Good question.

The truth is, all successfully married couples do just that: they try their own therapy at home. When they run into obstacles in their marriage, they do "therapy." That is, they look for actions, strategies, and information that can eliminate or at least minimize the difficulty.

If, somewhere along the way, this process is not working effectively, they might seek help. Help in doing what? In doing marriage therapy, of course. But the healing and development of their marriage still belongs to them.

Because we're the ones in our marriage, we're the only ones who can manage it. Our marriage is ours. It belongs to us. Are we qualified? Yes; in fact, we're the only ones truly qualified to manage our own lives.

WHAT ABOUT CREDENTIALS?

Dr. May delivers a remarkable insight on the subject of credentials: "Of all the questions I've been asked as a psychiatrist, the most common and disturbing ones have been about how to raise children. It has always seemed rather strange that people can expect psychiatric training to create an authority on child raising. It would make much more sense to search out a grandmother whose offspring are living fully and beautifully and ask her about it all."

What Dr. May recognizes is that we too often seek worldly credentials and forget common sense. Common sense would teach that successful living is itself a credential. Common sense would point out that schooling and education—though valuable in preparing us to live successfully—are not necessarily the same thing. How we live is up to us.

Similarly, how we handle our marriages is up to us as well. What we do to improve, develop, or ruin them is up to us. We're entitled to pick the tools and equipment we use to do repairs. We evaluate a problem or challenge and put together the plan to deal with it. The problem could be serious enough to require another point of view or some insight provided by a caring and competent counselor. Or maybe what's needed is the information and motivation to implement the changes ourselves. The focus is on getting on track, paying attention, and putting in the effort required to heal and grow.

Becoming Strong Together

That effort to heal, if you make it together, strengthens you and prepares you for the next challenge to come. This is the labor of love, which provides proof that you two together are capable of great things. The motivation for this work is love, commitment, and the faith that your union is valuable beyond earthly measure. The strength and courage required for this endeavor is to be found in the marriage, as it grows.

Ongoing effective marital therapy is a lot like any kind of maintenance, in these ways:

- It requires that we be responsive to real needs in real time.
- It must be ongoing, timely, and appropriate in scope.
- It can't be too cumbersome or slow, or it won't be effective.
- It must focus on specific (or at least limited) issues, or it will be too broad and won't accomplish anything.
- It needs to provide a way for the process to be ongoing in order to respond to our changing needs.

In other words, it needs to be brief, specific, and intermittent, as required.

This is the model that builds a marriage over time. Two properly motivated individuals will use the necessary resources to improve their marriage. They'll combine their skills, talents, and energies to overcome obstacles in their path. This is the purpose of all you've read and discussed so far.

The challenges of life that you have overcome in the living of it have prepared you for this great opportunity called marriage. The process that is marriage is all about the daily victories and challenges that teach us to build, learn, enjoy, and struggle together.

THE STRAW THAT BROKE THE CAMEL'S BACK

We are all familiar with the saying "That's the last straw," or "That's the straw that broke the camel's back." Many couples come into counseling with the last straw as the thing they want to talk about. The problem is how she squeezes the toothpaste tube or how he chews. It is the last little thing that has made the load too heavy to bear.

But there is a flaw in this last-straw thinking. What we forget is that the weight of every part of the load comes to bear. We focus on the last but not necessarily the heaviest thing. We look at the final straw but not the forty pounds of bricks it is resting on.

What we need to do is come up with a plan to reduce the whole load, not just remove the last straw. This should begin with what we need to carry least. Many concentrate on the most visible, not the heaviest or least useful part of the load. If we see a bridge sign that says the safe limit is five tons, we should not try ten and hope for the best; we should stop and take the load down to the safe limit before going on.

We all have limits to what we can carry. We need to consider those limits when we are planning how to live. We need to consider the safe load for ourselves and for our spouse before we just keep piling up more and hope for the best. This means discussing the load and being willing to look at what is necessary and what is not. It also means planning.

I have a friend who is a city planner; his job is to make sure the city doesn't spend more than it can afford. To do this, he matches projected revenue streams with the city's projected expenditures, planning a budget that is well below expected revenues. In the process, he will allow for unidentified but expected challenges. They are expected because experience has taught him that, as the common folk wisdom states, "Stuff happens."

The same is true of marriage. We must look at what has to be done and apply our resources, our carrying power if you will, to the tasks. We must recognize that we can't carry everything safely. Nobody can do everything. We must plan our loads carefully, making allowances for those extra challenges that experience teaches us will come. This is the way to keep that little straw in our relationship from getting so much attention it causes us to overlook the real load.

START TO PLAN

The basic cornerstone of improving marital communication may be a weekly planning meeting. It starts couples talking, and the benefit in time and energy is easy to see. Consider the benefits of a brief weekly meeting to combine your calendars for the coming week. This puts you in an unemotional environment to discuss the simplest kind of life improvement, better use of your time. Effective time and resource management begins with scheduling. A simple, thirty-minute meeting can save hours of phone and driving time for a family each week. (We hold ours on Sunday night.) Such a meeting also allows you to start some mutually beneficial problem solving. It gets you talking. It requires time together and opens the door for more and better cooperation. Consider the following components for a scheduling meeting:

- Hold the meeting weekly.
- Keep it short—approximately thirty minutes.
- Review day-by-day family activities and requirements—ball games, lessons, church activities, school activities, trips to the airport, company dinners, and so on.
- Schedule time to spend together.
- Discuss and schedule projects or activities you would like to do.

- Discuss how the children are doing, or mention something positive about each other.

Such a meeting will not only save hours but also set the stage for removing fear over talking about change.

CREATING AN EFFECTIVE DISCUSSION ENVIRONMENT

If you decide to improve your marriage, you'll need to talk to each other about your marriage. As obvious as this sounds, not making time for communication has kept many marriages from improving. What can we do to create the best possible environment for effective communication about our marriage? We need to have a meeting of the minds and hearts that follows some simple guidelines:

- Schedule a time to talk. As busy as our lives are, we need to make time for the things that matter most. Talking about our lives together is one of those things.
- Schedule a starting and ending time. As with any other meeting, an "open-ended" time frame can be interpreted as "endless." The thought of such an undefined meeting may make you or your spouse uncomfortable.
- Don't meet when emotions are running high regarding the topic of discussion. For example, when you've just discovered the checking account is overdrawn is not the time to discuss improving financial communications in your marriage. Solve the current problem as best you can and then come

back to the big picture later, after emotions have stabilized.

- Decide on a topic. The list of possible topics for discussion is endless. That can be frightening, too, if you see this time together as an endless series of what is wrong with us—or you. It's essential to see this as your planning time, your growing time, a time for the two of you. You can talk about vacation plans, scheduling, and the needs of family and friends. And you'll still have time to learn, improve, and heal, if necessary.

Why is being married a high priority for you both? One of the first times you meet, that could be a topic of great value. What is your motivation to improve? How does developing a wonderful marriage pay off for each of you?

Meet consistently. Even brief, specific, constructive conversations held consistently over time can yield great benefits. Think of these discussions as preventive maintenance. Ongoing care and attention can prevent the need for a major overhaul or even replacement.

Meeting together doesn't take the place of a date. The time you spend together courting and doing fun things is essential to mental and marital health. We're talking about finding time to learn about and plan how to be married more effectively; a time to turn stumbling blocks into stepping stones; a time to grow, to learn, and to heal; a time to become self-directed. This is the time to choose and chart your path together to the eternal city, our eternal home.

I'm encouraged by the words of a great teacher. Gandhi said, "A small body of determined spirits fired by an unquenchable faith in their mission can alter the course of history."

Introduction to Skills

I mentioned before the simple Latin phrase "Nam et ipsa scientia potestas est," attributed to Englishman Sir Francis Bacon. It's one of my favorite quotations about learning.

Bacon was a native English speaker, but he chose Latin to express his belief that knowledge is power. This simple, direct statement is made even more powerful by his use of Latin, which was at that time the language of learning. How? As one who doesn't speak Latin, I cannot understand what is being said without a translator. Therefore, I don't have the power to understand, because I don't have the knowledge to translate. Bacon uses the language of the declaration itself to powerfully illustrate his point. Yes, knowledge is power!

This applies to most of what we deal with in life. Knowing how to do a thing demystifies it. Having an understanding of a process or skill can make the seemingly impossible possible. In fact, many times what has become second nature to us, in our work or avocations, when observed by others, seems impossible. What we do with practice as a matter of course seems to the unskilled observer miraculous.

A DIFFICULT UPGRADE

Many years ago, while serving as a missionary in New Mexico, I lived in a small trailer behind a trading post on the Navajo reservation. The trader there was a native Californian. He was an engineer by training and was a passionate ham-radio operator. On those cold, clear reservation nights, this brother would expand the world he lived in by talking to people all over the globe from the trading post at Coyote Canyon, New Mexico.

As spring approached, he decided to upgrade his system. This was not only before the Internet but also before home computers or even VCRs, just about the time solid-state circuitry was coming into its own. His radio was a baffling array of what seemed like miles of wires and hundreds of tubes. As his radio upgrade started, he signed off for the last time on the old system.

He then began cannibalizing his old radio and integrating it into the new improved version of "Radio Reservation." For him, it was heavenly. At the end of each workday he'd retreat to the back room to work on his project. One night my companion and I needed to talk to him. We were ushered into the radio room with a knowing warning—"Don't touch anything"—spoken by his wife as we entered. If I live to be a hundred, that moment will live brightly etched in my nonmechanical mind.

Now, I'm the kind of person who won't buy anything that even suggests some assembly is required. As we stepped into that room, I saw the closest thing to hades that my nonengineering mind could fathom. There before me were wall-to-wall wires, tubes, dials, and meters of every description. In the middle of the room, sitting on the floor, shirtsleeves rolled up and special magnifying glasses tilted skyward, was the trader. He held a smoking soldering gun like some futuristic techno-gunfighter.

I was overcome, as I still am. The complexity of the task I saw spread out in that room was beyond my power to comprehend. The trader rose and came over to us smiling—smiling, mind you! We did whatever business we were there to do and started to leave. I bravely asked a parting question, something sensitive and intellectual like, "What would possess a fairly intelligent man like you to embark on a hideous project like this?"

He paused, smiled, and taught me one of the greatest lessons I've ever learned. "The reason this seems so complicated to you," he said, "is that you don't understand it. Every wire in here has only two ends. If you take it one wire at a time, it's that simple."

Whenever life gives me a new task or challenge, I just go back to that night in Coyote Canyon, New Mexico. I try to remember that my task is difficult because I don't understand it. Then I sit down or kneel down and take the time to find the first wire and decide where it goes, and one wire at a time, most things get done.

The skills we develop, our life experiences, and the lessons we take from those experiences are the tools we can use to identify which wires to look for or to look out for.

CHAPTER 9

Health and Rest

A dead thing can go with the stream, but only a living thing can go against it.
—G. K. Chesterton

When you're considering putting in the effort required to improve your partnership, make sure no physical limitation is keeping you or your spouse from being successful. Healthy people make better partners. Vince Lombardi, legendary NFL coach, said, "Fatigue makes cowards of us all." The essence of this and other similar comments is that our physical condition is often a major influence on our mental, spiritual, and emotional health.

We're familiar with postpartum depression, PMS, diabetes, and other debilitating influences. Chronic fatigue, depression, and a number of other equally dangerous conditions can also change the ability of even the most courageous spouse to contribute positively to a relationship. Many debilitating physical conditions might go unnoticed as affecting our mental, spiritual, and emotional well-being, if we don't know what to look for.

Make sure you consider any unusual behavioral patterns in you or your partner as a potential health issue. Inconsistent or changed behavior may be a medical issue, not an issue with your relationship. To find out for sure, get competent professional help. Yearly physicals, including blood and cardiovascular tests, are important parts of preventative health care.

HEALTHY PEOPLE MAKE HEALTHY MATES

A counseling client of mine, a former bishop, had a wonderful job and family, and he was simply a great guy. He came to my home office. There's a big old comfortable oak rocker in the corner, and he plopped down in it. The arms on that rocker are large and rounded on the front. Your hands can lie on them easily. He rested his hands on the arms of that old chair, and his fingers hung limply over the front edge.

After he'd been sitting a minute or two, I noticed sweat dripping from the tips of his fingers. He wasn't moving, and he hadn't been exercising. He was working so hard at being depressed that he was perspiring profusely. He was soaking wet. As we sat and talked, he said he hadn't slept for four or five days—he couldn't exactly remember. I asked him, "What are you feeling like?"

He said, "Well, I just want to kill myself."

One of the first things I was taught as a counseling student was how to confirm if people are really suicidal. The technique is to try to shock them about what they've just said or done that causes concern, using direct and very emotional language. The idea is to see what level of natural abhorrence they have for the thought of ending their own lives.

"How are you going to kill yourself?" I asked.

He said, "I was thinking a hose from the tail pipe to the window of my car would do it." He said this flatly, with no emotion at all. The thought of taking his own life held little or no emotion for him. He was just too hopeless and just too tired to care.

We stayed together until we got him to a hospital for further evaluation. They whacked him full of sedatives, and he mostly slept for three or four days. When he woke up, most of his depression was gone. Why he had become depressed isn't important here. What's important is that he'd been caught in kind of a downward emotional and physiological spiral and was ready to commit suicide. This very real challenge to his life was a physical manifestation of an emotional problem. It needed physical and emotional intervention. Why? Because depression kills people. It can be as serious as cancer or heart disease. Depression is literally life-threatening. What is more serious than that?

PHYSICAL AND EMOTIONAL CARE

Changes in body chemistry or condition can cause major problems. Consider this story related to me by Lisa, a building manager for a major corporation. She's bright, competent, and in good physical condition, but she has trouble keeping up her level of potassium. And when she doesn't get enough potassium, she gets paranoid and hallucinates.

She, her husband Ron, and several friends decided to take a day hike on Mount Rainier in Washington state. After several hours of hiking on a hot summer day, without realizing it, she'd become very low on potassium. She began to think that Ron and the others were plotting to kill her. She planned to save herself by finding a place on the trail to dump her pack and lose them in the woods. And she did just that.

Ron and the others saw Lisa dump her pack and run screaming into the woods. After a stunned moment or two, Ron and the others took up pursuit. Lisa, fearing for her life, hid from them successfully. Search and rescue dogs found her some time later passed out near a small creek bed. Within a few hours, with the proper care, she was back to normal. The lesson is that our physiology can have drastic effects on our behavior and even our safety.

SICK AND TIRED

One of the most common physical problems in our fast-paced Western world is chronic fatigue. As a population, we're tired a lot. When reported to a physician or counselor, this fatigue is often described in statements like these:

- "Something is wrong with me; I'm tired all the time."
- "We're just not interested in sex anymore. By the time we get a minute alone, all we want to do is sleep."
- "We don't have fun like we used to. The spark is gone from our lives."
- "I hate to go to work, so every Sunday night I get depressed."
- "By Friday night, I'm exhausted."

These comments and a thousand more like them indicate a need for rest, which is important in rejuvenating our physical bodies.

Exercise: Why Are We So Tired?

To work on improving your marriage, one of the first things you should do is assess your physical health and its effect on your lives. Discuss these topics for possible areas in which you might be doing some harm. Add any others you can think of. Brainstorm possible ways to minimize the impact of these issues and note them in the section that follows.

What stresses are ongoing in your lives? (School, work, children, family demands, and so on.)

Do you or a close family member have any long-term illnesses?

Are you (individually) getting enough sleep?

Are you taking any medication that might be a problem?

Are you living with a family member or friend?

How is work going?

Have you moved or are you considering a move?

When was your last physical examination?

Is there a pattern to your emotional ups and downs?

How are your finances?

WHAT CAN BE DONE?

Most physical stresses can be reduced if we identify them effectively and adjust in the ways that are possible. Even the most difficult ones—such as the long-term illness of a child or spouse, or the death of a loved one—can be better handled if we've identified the potential these experiences carry for related health problems.

Forewarned is forearmed. The important thing is to be proactive in eliminating or at least minimizing the effects of these problems. Here are a few things you can do to restore your fatigue-deprived health:

• Find time to schedule a nap together.

- Trade baby-sitting with a friend so you can get some time alone to rest.
- Arrange for time together away from home.
- Get appropriate medical care as needed.
- Make an effort to exercise.
- Eat regular and balanced meals.
- Be aware of and sensitive to the needs of your spouse. (If there's a time of day, week, or month where one or the other of you needs to be particularly kind or sensitive to the other, do so.)

King Benjamin recognized the connection between physical and spiritual well-being when he counseled, "See that all . . . things are done in wisdom and order; for it is not requisite that a man should run faster than he has strength. And again, it is expedient that he should be diligent, that thereby he might win the prize; therefore, all things must be done in order" (Mosiah 4:27).

The Lord gave the same admonition to the Prophet Joseph regarding the translation of the Book of Mormon: "Do not run faster or labor more than you have strength and means provided to enable you to translate; but be diligent unto the end" (D&C 10:4).

Whatever the consideration, remember the principle: Healthy people make healthy relationships. In practical terms, sometimes a two-hour nap is the best way to avoid a four-hour fight!

CHAPTER 10

Recommitting

Knowing is not enough; we must apply. Willing is not enough; we must do.
—Goethe

$\mathcal{I}$f you were meeting your spouse for the first time, what would you do to interest him or her in you? One strategy I often suggest is as effective as it is fun: Think of a way to get your spouse to want to go out with you. That's right, do the very thing that you did in the beginning. Put together a plan to have your spouse become interested in you as possible date material.

In my case, for example, that might mean bringing home a note or flowers. Perhaps I'll ask my wife if she would like to go get a milk shake some evening. I could use the talking time to help her understand what a great guy I am. I might even mention what a great person *she* is. We could talk about things we both found interesting. This talk would serve as the opportunity to prove myself fun enough to merit consideration for a full-blown date. Getting to know your spouse the first time was great fun. Do it again.

My wife has often said that many people seem willing to do things to interest or accommodate a second mate that would have kept the first one. Remember what it was that started it all for you.

Was she important?

She still is.

Was being in love fun?

It still is.

Exercise: Would You Be Interested Now?

Plan with your spouse some ways you might interest each other if you were meeting for the first time. Then implement your plan. At the least, take a moment to discuss the following questions:

- What was it about you that first attracted me?
- What was it about me that first attracted you?
- What kept your interest?
- What kept my interest?
- What did we do that was enjoyable?
- What do we do now that is enjoyable and interesting?

- Here is how you have grown and changed in ways that I admire.
- What can we do to have an interesting and fun time together?

TEN COMMANDMENTS FOR
BUILDING A CELESTIAL MARRIAGE

May I suggest ten commandments for building a celestial marriage? They are simple, not spectacular. But they're helpful in evaluating your level of commitment.

There's a sermon for yourself in every one. If you take the time to review and ponder them, they will provide a benchmark for measuring the current condition of your relationship. They might also give you some areas to consider for future growth.

- Spend time together.
- Speak kindly.
- Laugh often.
- Touch gently.
- Be patient.
- Sustain each other.
- Play together.
- Be committed.
- Listen respectfully.
- Be interested.

Exercise: Implementing the Ten Commandments

With your spouse, separately list the ten commandments for building a celestial marriage in order of their importance to you. Then discuss your lists together. You may find that although you both recognize the value in all the statements, how you value each one may be a little different. This exercise will help you discover what each of you consider to be important, and why. Knowing what your mate values most from the list will help you be more effective in building your relationship.

During your discussion, talk about what each commandment means to you and how you do or could apply them. For example:

- How can I show you I'm committed to you in a way you'll recognize and feel good about?
- What time am I spending with you that lets you know you're important to me?
- What time do we spend together that we find enjoyable?
- How can I sustain and support you in doing what you enjoy or feel is important?
- What could we do to have more fun together?
- How could I better demonstrate my interest in you?

Take time to learn by listening to each other about how to build your marriage. Invest the effort to find out not only what you can do to demonstrate your commitment to your spouse but also to trust your spouse enough to share what he or she can do to help you feel appreciated. The rewards will be worth the effort.

CHAPTER 11

Agreement versus Understanding

Friendship that insists upon agreement on all matters is not worth the name. Friendship to be real must ever sustain the weight of honest differences, however sharp they be.
—*Mohandas Gandhi*

There's a recurring misunderstanding in relationships that often leads to the most impassable of arguments. Battle lines get drawn, and productive movement ceases. This misunderstanding is at the root of great debates, and it has led to murder and even war. It has been at the root of holy wars for centuries. The principle we need to grasp and apply in our relationships, especially those we want to last, is: *Agreement and understanding are not the same thing.*

Many of us don't see agreement and understanding as different. But thinking they are leads to a logical but problematic assumption: "If you really understood my

118

position, you'd agree with me." Unfortunately, that statement is based on some other pretty negative assumptions. It implies that if you don't agree with me, you must be:

- too stubborn to admit you're wrong.
- intentionally ignoring the truth.
- needing to have things explained again, better, so that even *you* can understand.

This final assumption has led and continues to lead to endless unproductive and frustrating marathons of marital madness.

CAN WE IN GOOD FAITH DISAGREE?

This basic misunderstanding has been particularly evident and destructive in the history of religion. A groundbreaking book coauthored by Steven E. Robinson and Craig Bloomberg addresses the problem of understanding and agreement wonderfully. The book, *How Wide the Divide,* represents the perspectives of evangelical Christians and Latter-day Saints on several doctrinal issues.

Their discussion is designed to foster understanding and mutual respect. They present their positions with passion, intellectual precision, and (for the most part) spiritual clarity. Here are two bright, well-educated men who have made Christian doctrinal understanding and insight their life's work. Both seem well-intentioned and sincere. How is it possible that they disagree?

A quotation from the book illustrates how they went

about dealing with the difference between understanding and agreement. They're talking here about how to change the way they look at their disagreements in order to be less offensive and more constructive. They refer to the need to see each other as reasonable and well-intentioned people: "This changes the discussion from—I'm right and no one who believes otherwise can do so without rejecting the Bible—(which both sides find insulting) to *I grant that things could in good faith be interpreted your way. I do not believe it's the correct interpretation, however.*"

While it's obvious that they still do not agree, they have framed their discussion in such a way as to sow the seeds of understanding.

Understanding Is Essential

Here's a rule of thumb for applying this principle in your marriage. Remember that agreement, though pleasant, is not always necessary. But understanding is essential. Understanding is required for a harmonious and mutually respectful relationship. For my part, understanding means I've taken the time to listen and really hear you. Even though we may still disagree, I was respectful enough to hear your opinion and value it as you have mine.

This may prove more difficult in practice than it sounds in principle. It hasn't crossed some of our minds that two perfectly sane and normal people can view the same issue differently. It has also not occurred to many that this can be done while both partners are on solid intellectual and moral ground. There are various words and phrases that can be a tip-off that one or the other of you might not quite understand the concept, or at least isn't applying it yet. They may sound something like this:

- "If she really understood my point she'd agree with me."
- "He's just got to be right, no matter what."

That need to be right demonstrates lack of understanding and an emphasis on the need for agreement.

All too often someone introduces a new element: "You just don't understand how I feel." That may be true, but he just wants to know what she *thinks*—especially if she has "come to her senses" and agrees with him.

"What do you mean you don't care how I feel?" she queries, feeling hurt and devalued. He wonders (now confused beyond belief), "When did this become a conversation about feelings? Who let that ugly monster in the door? We were talking about whether or not I'm right, not how you *feel* about whether or not I'm right."

Such a circular nightmare of misinformation, misunderstanding, and defensive posturing can continue forever. Think of all the precious time wasted in trying to figure out what just happened.

Frankly, most of what we fight about doesn't matter much in the overall picture. Unless we take the time to understand, we're only focusing on not agreeing. When the need to prove or defend our idea becomes so important, we often forget what we were talking about before the point became who's right and who's wrong.

Seeking Understanding

Seeking understanding has enormous power. It can change the very fabric of our relationship. When we focus on understanding, agreement is still possible but not required. The whole aim of the exchange moves from mere persuasion to true communication.

Many times good communication can help educate us, allowing us to modify our position willingly. That's right—good communication (in a nondefensive, nonoffensive way) can also persuade. And it helps lead to more profound insights and blessings.

For example, let's suppose I get home from work and see my wife engaged in some project. I say, "Honey, you look tired; let me help you finish." She bursts into tears and tells me how insensitive I am. If I then focus on proving that she is wrong and that I am sensitive and caring even if I have to crush her to be that way, the situation deteriorates into combat. On the other hand, if her interpretation of my comment seems inconsistent with my intended message, perhaps I should find out why. The conversation might go like this:

"I'm sorry if my comment hurt your feelings. That surely was not my intention. I was hoping to help so you could get a break. What did I say that hurt your feelings?"

"Well, I know I look ugly today, and I was trying to

get this all done and look a little better before you got home. It is taking a lot longer than I thought it would, and I'm sure you could do a much better job at it than I am."

What I said was, "Honey, you look tired; let me help you finish." What she heard was, "You are ugly and incompetent." There was no way to anticipate this interpretation from her, but by listening with an open heart and mind, I can learn that what I think I said may not be what she heard. In this case, perhaps I can help her understand that "tired" and "ugly" are not the same for me. She might even come to understand that I am trying to be sensitive to the heavy load she carries. Seeking to understand gives us both an opportunity to learn. As one of my clients said, "I don't know if my husband really agrees with me, but at least he took the time to hear me out, ask good questions, and listen. He was respectful."

Caring enough to listen to your mate, to share your thoughts and feelings, is the beginning of true intimacy. That intimacy demonstrates the respect you have for your spouse and awakens trust. It does not always lead to agreement, but (done with honest interest) it generally leads to peace.

CHAPTER 12

Communication Skills

To keep your marriage brimming
With love in the wedding cup,
Whenever you're wrong, admit it;
Whenever you're right, shut up.

—Ogden Nash

Experts in communication have a saying that demonstrates how complex communication can be: "The one thing we know about communication is that it never occurs." As cynical as this seems, it can help us avoid being frustrated when a message we give or receive is somehow not effective.

If we believe the myth that when we hear we understand completely, and when we speak we're understood completely, we're doomed to a life of frustration and defeat in our communication. The reality is that most of us communicate enough information to get by. And most of the time, that's enough. However, as information becomes more complex, the amount of material that needs to be communicated becomes ever greater.

Any message we receive in any format passes through what communications experts have called our "perceptual filters." What that means is, we interpret messages in the context of our total life experience—language, history, gender, education, work experience, family background, cultural training, social norms, and so on. In short, who we are determines how we hear, see, feel, read, or experience the messages we receive.

MIND-READER COMMUNICATION

Let me illustrate with an example of what we laughingly refer to in our house as mind-reader communication. When we were first married, Lois believed that husbands (hers in particular) should know what wives (her in particular) were thinking. She can't remember being taught this, but nonetheless it was there.

The concept goes something like this: "He is the husband, and he will know what the wife needs. If I have to ask for things, he isn't paying attention. In fact, that might be proof that he doesn't even love me."

As a young married man, I came home to our little apartment and was greeted at the door by my beaming wife with this question—a question, by the way, that many others have reported hearing. She asked, "Do you notice anything different?" I was speechless as my two options became obvious to me:

I am such an insensitive pig that I did not notice.

I noticed but am such an insensitive pig that I did not mention it.

Such traps have led to many no-win arguments. May I suggest a simple plan for a healthy "notice-and-be-noticed" solution? Lois and I have a deal. If she wants me to notice something, she points it out and asks, "What do you think?" Novel, huh! I can then respond in an honest and informed way. The arrangement is the same if I need her to notice something or give me an opinion.

There is a difference, of course, between "I need some attention for this" and "What is your opinion of what I did?" Men, as the problem-solving gender, need to pay particular attention to the fact that there is a difference.

Here's another example of this unproductive, mind-reader communication. A husband, noticing his wife's crestfallen countenance, asks, "Honey, is something wrong?" She responds, "If you are so insensitive that you don't know, then I am not going to tell you!"

Don't make me guess what is hurting you, even if I have been the cause of such hurt. If I am to offer a comforting spirit or begin meaningful repentance, I must know what you are experiencing and why. I suggest the same straightforward type of solution as before: Share what you are feeling. Expect that your partner wants to offer a listening ear and heart. Allow your friend in marriage to express that friendship in kindness, in your time of need.

We need to begin the process of receiving what we need from our spouse by developing the faith and trust to communicate those needs. As a partner, we must also cultivate the faith and trust to gently receive such communication. Giving and receiving in this way encourages growth. Revealing ourselves and our desires in such an environment brings us closer and develops our ability to help and be helped by the one we have chosen to be with forever.

The same is true for any message we send. We craft our communication based on our personal experience. Because no two people are exactly alike, we all communicate differently. Every message passes through the perceptual filters of the sender and the receiver. The receiver evaluates the message, decides how to craft a response, and sends it back through his or her filters and yours. Every exchange passes through each person's perceptual filters twice, once to send and once to receive. That is repeated for every exchange in every communication.

Discuss with your spouse how your perceptual filters may affect your communication with each other, your families, people at work, and anybody else you communicate with. Remember, it is not only your filters you need to be aware of but your partner's as well. Understanding the impact of context (the perception of both sender and receiver) on communication is a huge milestone in understanding how to improve your effectiveness as a communicator, in both sending and receiving information.

Consider the complexity of business or real-estate contracts. The documents required to substantiate our verbal agreements are voluminous. Consider the technical manuals required for computer software. Have you ever struggled with the assembly instructions for a child's bike or a relatively simple piece of furniture? The cliché of a leftover nut or bolt or an extra, seemingly crucial piece after the project is assembled has become a running gag synonymous with self-assembled projects.

But compared to the infinite variables of a lifelong, dynamic marriage, these contracts and instructions are kid's stuff. When it comes to communicating with your mate, good basic skills will help make the process more effective and hopefully less frustrating and painful.

If it's true that perfect communication never happens, we're forced to ask, "What, then, can we hope to achieve?" The answer must be, "We seek to be as effective and efficient in our communication with each other as possible." Effective means getting the information across in the most complete form we can. Efficient means doing it in an acceptable time frame.

We're busy people, and we don't have an infinite amount of time to check and recheck our messages to each other. So the relation between quality of message and understanding must of necessity be balanced with the time available to deliver and receive our messages.

Assumptions Can Be Damaging

Communication is the key to understanding. When we simply *assume* that we know what our partner is thinking, we invite disaster.

Dave and Carrie had been married more than thirty

years. They had raised a successful family and were "empty-nesters" in their third or fourth year with no children at home. After a brief, unemotional discussion on the matter, they decided to divorce.

They never fought, and they were model citizens and good people. After a fruitless discussion with their kids, they reluctantly agreed to visit a counselor before starting divorce proceedings. The first session was quiet, with both partners agreeing that divorce was their only option. Dave cited the fact that his wife didn't love him as his reason for the breakup. Carrie's reason was exactly the same, from the other side: "He just doesn't love me."

They agreed they had stayed together for the children but could no longer deal with being unloved. Conspicuously absent, however, were the phrases "I don't love her" and "I don't love him." Each agreed to meet with the counselor alone to discuss the pain they were experiencing in this situation.

Dave was a blue-collar worker who had risen to management responsibilities in a local utility company. He was quiet and capable and seemed reasonable almost to a fault. When asked to describe what he and Carrie had fought about that led to the decision to divorce, his answer was surprising: "We've never fought much. I know we don't always agree, but we work things out pretty well." He went on to explain that Carrie was the finest woman he'd ever known. She was kind and tolerant, a good mother and faithful wife. She was a great cook and kept a fine house. He described her as an ideal partner for him. At a loss to understand what was going on, the counselor asked why he'd divorce such a woman. He answered as before, "She just doesn't love me, and I can't take it anymore. I love her so much, but she doesn't love me."

"How do you know?" asked the counselor. Dave's answer was startling. "We've been married for more than thirty years. I've gotten up every morning at four-thirty to go to work to support her and the kids, and she has never once gotten up to make me breakfast."

Had Dave told Carrie he wanted breakfast in the morning?

"No. If she doesn't care enough to make it, I guess I don't need to beg." He went on to tell of his youth on a dairy farm. His mother, who loved his dad so much, got up every morning to fix him a "good, big, farm breakfast" to see him through the day. Mom would then go back to bed, and Dad and the boys were careful not to go near the house until after noon so Mom could get her proper rest.

"It's not that I don't want Carrie to rest. I never call home to bother her sleep. But she just doesn't care enough to get up, and I can't take it anymore." That was that. Dave was done.

Carrie's appointment followed the next day. The same questions brought similar results. She had great love and respect for her husband. In her eyes, Dave was a kind man, a good provider and father. She loved him but could no longer stand his obvious lack of love for her.

"How do you know Dave doesn't love you?" the counselor asked. Carrie's answer was clear: "For more than thirty years he's left for work in a thunder of noise. He rattles pans when he makes his breakfast, and he slams the door when he leaves. It's as if Dave is trying to make getting any rest impossible. I know he wants me to get up and make him breakfast. If he really loved me, he'd want me to sleep.

"Dave doesn't even call me in the day," she went on, "to see how I'm doing. My father had a grocery delivery route, and he left the house early every morning. He loved my mother with all his heart. She was fragile and often sick, so she needed her rest. He'd sneak out of the house and never make a peep. He couldn't stand being away from her, so about mid-morning, when he was sure she was awake, he'd call to check in on her. That's the kind of thing a man who loves his wife does."

Here were two good people who loved each other. They had missed out on years of feeling loved because they had never discussed with each other what love meant to them. They had ignored successes in every aspect of their lives to concentrate on feeling unloved about breakfast.

The good news is that the outcome for this couple was very positive. When faced with what was going on, they were able to reach a compromise in minutes. The bad news is the years of joy that were missed because they hadn't taken time to talk about their needs.

HOW CAN WE BETTER COMMUNICATE?

There are several skills that can help you better communicate with each other. Organization, problem-solving and decision-making skills, questioning skills, and listening skills all contribute to quality two-way communication.

To be effective in using these tools, you must accept some basic assumptions that will help you establish an environment for communication.

These assumptions will help only if you honestly agree on them. If you don't, now is a good time to start improving the way you communicate. If, for example,

---

Exercise: Setting Up Some Assumptions

Take some time to look at the following assumptions and come to an understanding that your communication will take place in a safe environment. Agreeing in advance to these basic assumptions—and sticking with them—will help avoid needless hurt and confusion.

- I'll never purposely say or do anything to hurt you.
- It's never my intention to make you look or feel stupid or foolish.
- I understand that misunderstandings and miscommunications occur, and the difficulty can be in either sending or receiving the message.

- Who's at fault in a misunderstanding or mis-communication isn't important. The objective is to clear up miscommunication, learn from it, improve future interaction, and move forward.
- I'm always free to ask questions if I feel that the message is not yet clear or I want to con-firm my understanding. Questions are not intended to make either of us feel incompetent or stupid.
- Asking for or giving written instructions or reminders is okay. It's not an admission or accu-sation of forgetfulness, incompetence, or stupidity.

you *do* intend to communicate in a way that will hurt your spouse, that will make suspect any communication you attempt.

Maybe you believe that anyone who needs written instructions is an idiot. If so, you need to know that we all learn and process information differently, regardless of the level of our intelligence.

The point here is simple. If we can get the basic assumptions about our intentions out of the way and just try to be more effective communicators, our chances of improving are dramatically increased.

CHAPTER 13

Questioning: A Tool for Mutual Understanding

The capacity for delight is the gift of paying attention.
—Julia Cameron

The secret of craftsmanship is knowing which tool serves what purpose, and then using that tool for the job it was designed to do. Think of questions as tools for intelligent and caring communication.

There are two kinds of questions that we'll explore in this chapter: open and closed. You may already be familiar with these, possibly under different names. For example, open questions have been referred to as nondirective or illustrative questions. Closed questions have been called directed, specific, or limiting questions.

Whatever names they go by, these two simple questioning forms are the basic building blocks of inquiry.

Both open and closed questions can provide valuable information. You just need to know how and when to use them. Each type of question serves a purpose, and they're often asked in sequence.

CLOSED QUESTIONS

Closed questions are used for getting specific information as effectively as possible. They are asked in such a way as to limit the possible responses to brief and definitive answers. "Yes" or "no" questions are by definition closed questions, aiming at a limited, specific response. But they're not the only types of closed questions. Here are some other examples of closed questions. Their utility should be obvious:

- Who is that person? (aims at a specific name and/or identifying description)
- What do you want to do about the tire, repair it or replace it? (aims at a specific, limited choice)
- When will your plane arrive? (limited to a specific date and/or time)
- Where is the shut-off valve? (aimed at a specific locality and/or direction)
- Did the car break down because of the radiator? (aimed at a specific confirmation of a cause)
- How much do I owe you? (aimed at a specific amount)

These questions are closed because they lead to a specific, limited answer. In other words, they confirm the inquirer's knowledge or understanding of a single point.

Much of what we need to know is very precise. Closed questions are the easiest and most effective way to get that kind of information.

Open Questions

Open questions elicit more information or greater complexity in their response. By their nature, open questions encourage the respondent to tell more than closed questions do. They often ask someone to describe, illustrate, or explain, and they can be directive statements we respond to as if they were questions. If a question can be answered by "yes" or "no," it's not open. Here are some examples:

- Who are some of the people we need to consider for this position?
- What went on at work today?
- When in your career did you feel like this training was useful?
- How did you solve the problem?
- Where in the process could such a thing possibly happen?
- Give me an illustration.
- Why do you suppose they restructured the department?
- Explain how you handled that.
- How do you feel about the changes in the updated word-processing software?
- Describe the project for me.
- Give me an example of what to expect.

SOME REALITIES OF QUESTIONING

One roadblock to effective communication is that we get in the habit of asking closed questions when we really want to ask open ones. For example:

Q: Could you tell me what is wrong? (Closed question.)

A: Yes. (Closed response.)

We also find ourselves answering open questions with closed answers, and closed questions with open responses. Here are some examples:

Q: What went on today at work? (Open question.)

A: Nothing. (Closed response.)

Q: Was your vacation fun? (Closed question.)

A: You can't even imagine how much fun. First day out, the weather was just horrible, and I thought we were doomed. But we found some of the most wonderful little shops to browse around in. We met a very interesting couple from Spain, of all places, and . . . (Open response.)

In practical terms, we get by pretty well by guessing the intent of the person asking the question and responding accordingly. Though this answer-by-assumption method of communicating generally works, there's a more effective way.

When we ask more effectively what we want to know, two things happen. First, we take the time to decide just what it is we really want to understand. Second, we listen more intently. This sensitivity to questions and answers makes us better communicators as questioners, and better listeners when the other person is responding.

The Need to Talk and Listen

We must communicate if we want to understand our differences as well as the things we have in common. Asking questions is valuable as each of us begins to discover who our partner is. The reason for developing this skill is that questioning is essential to good communication. And good communication is a key to making misunderstandings as infrequent as possible. We may assume that we understand what has been said, but that's not always the case. We must develop an attitude that encourages and accommodates questions. This is especially important if we feel that what we're hearing isn't making sense.

For example, when your spouse asks, "Do you want to go to the movies tonight?" is that an invitation or a request for your preference? Is your spouse saying, "I'd like to go to the movies; would you like to come with me?" or "Do you feel like going to the movies?" Either one could be the case.

A friend of mine recently discovered, after more than thirty years of marriage, that he'd been rejecting his wife's invitations for years because he thought she was asking for his preference. Consider how she felt when she would ask him, "Do you want to go to the movies tonight?" and he would just say, "No"—not even "No, thank you," but just "No."

She finally asked why he always refused her invitation. He responded, "What invitation?" He had thought she was asking if he felt like going to the movies, not inviting him to go with her. This little misunderstanding was cleared up as a result of that single question, but thirty years of unintentional hurt could have been avoided if the question had been asked much earlier.

We need to confirm that what we're hearing or feeling is an accurate reflection of what our spouse is actually trying to communicate. We also need to accept the fact that our differences are not necessarily issues of right or wrong; most of the time, they're just differences. You might think one way, and your spouse might think another. Your way might be as effective for you as your spouse's way is for him or her. Who knows, you might even learn something from each other!

Understanding fosters self-disclosure, and self-disclosure is the key to true intimacy. If you take the time to lovingly understand and be understood, you'll draw as close as is possible here on earth. The joy of really knowing and trusting comes from understanding and feeling understood.

ENCOURAGING COMMUNICATION

Encouraging open communication between husband and wife educates the entire family. The couple is better off and more capable of coping with a broader array of information by using their skills and experiences as partners, not competitors.

A marriage, or any family unit, for that matter, can be referred to as an open system or a closed system. An open system is one that welcomes information, experience, and new concepts as learning opportunities to be valued and enjoyed. Closed systems, on the other hand, often see new or different ideas as a threat or challenge to the stability of the system. In a closed system, nothing is more valuable than the status quo. New information or any kind of change is frightening.

To illustrate the differences between open and closed systems, think of a marriage or family as a house. I like to picture a big old country farmhouse, a two-story white frame home overlooking beautiful fields of crops, with a verdant mountain valley beyond. The green fields are framed with white board fences, and a beautiful trout stream flows from the far blue mountains, running playfully through the yard.

If this house represents an open system, the windows are flung wide open on this beautiful summer day, inviting every bit of life and light in the universe inside.

If the house represents a closed system, the shutters are nailed shut and the curtains pulled tight, even though the summer day contains no threat. It makes no difference what the outside world looks like, because the people living there will never see it. The air inside is dank, and the light is so artificial that the limited spectrum illuminates only a few feet at a time.

For clarification, it's important to carry our little illustration one step further. We recognize that all outside influences are not healthy. For example, even in an open family system, the house would not have all the windows flung open at thirty degrees below zero. But I like to think of the open family system responding appropriately to the threatening weather outside. The fireplace would hold a cozy, warming fire, so the occupants could look on the outside world from the safety of the house and appreciate the sturdy old structure.

The point is, an open system would evaluate the outside world, recognize opportunity or threat, and respond accordingly. The threat of cold weather could also hold the opportunity of viewing a beautiful winter scene.

The closed structure would always assume the worst, taking any outside influence as a threat to be avoided. This assumption of ever-present threat limits our ability to receive the fresh, life-bringing air of summer and appreciate the cozy comfort of protection on a chilly winter day.

HOW CAN WE SEE OUR OPPORTUNITIES?

How do we see the opportunities that lie in the differences between us? How do we see the skills and gifts we each bring to the wedding feast? Can we accept the value of this diversity—embrace the breadth of the differences that both individuals bring to this union? Can we do this without asking whose talent is more valuable in today's marketplace?

Which of the houses we spoke of—closed or open— best represents the condition of your heart? Are the windows of your heart and mind open to the beauty and potential of your mate? Are your heart and mind open to your own beauty and potential?

Are we willing to learn and grow, to evaluate our lives and start again? If we are and if we do, the possibilities are as endless as the beauty and potential of a sunny summer day. Together our combined gifts, experiences, and talents bring limitless opportunity.

CHAPTER 14

Choosing How to Respond

We who lived in concentration camps can remember the men who walked through the huts comforting others, giving away their last piece of bread. They may have been few in number, but they offer sufficient proof that everything can be taken from a man but one thing: the last of the human freedoms—to choose one's attitude in any given set of circumstances.

—Victor Frankl

Most people are familiar with the Pavlovian model of conditioned response. Pavlov was the Russian scientist who used dogs as subjects in groundbreaking research in conditioned response. Science now recognizes that when a specific stimulus is provided to an animal (in the case of Pavlov's dogs, it was food), the animal will instinctively and predictably react to that stimulus. Pavlov's dogs' reaction was to salivate.

This predictable response is even observable in the one-celled amoeba. This simple organism will instinctively move away from an electrical prod—stimulus and response.

ANOTHER STEP FOR US

The stimulus-response model often applies to human beings as well as animals. But our ability to think and choose before we act makes the concept of stimulus-response a little different for us. As humans, we can make a conscious decision about our responses to the stimuli in our lives.

The war in heaven was fought over this right to choose. Our sacred obligation and opportunity to decide how we'll respond to the challenges and events of life was purchased at a high price indeed. It must be vitally important.

A favorite saying of mine suggests that life is 10 percent what happens to you and 90 percent what you do with it. In other words, how you choose to respond to life is up to you.

This principle of active participation in the outcome of our own lives is the very heart of this book. You have a choice of how you want your life to go. Being actively engaged in how you want your marriage to be is important. Freedom of choice is what separates us from the rest of the animal kingdom. This is God's gift to His children.

Henry David Thoreau put it beautifully when he said, "I know of no more encouraging fact than the unquestionable ability of man to elevate his life by conscious endeavor."

PREDICTING THE ACTIONS OF PEOPLE

Our ability to choose how we respond is what makes predicting human behavior so difficult. Some wonderful families produce rotten kids. Some families in the most difficult situations produce remarkable kids.

Although alcoholic parents have a higher-than-average number of alcoholic offspring (suggesting a possible physiological as well as sociological reason for alcoholism), some children from these families see the destructive results of alcoholism in their families and choose never to drink. That is true in my case.

The great revelation and freeing principle here is that the past doesn't have to equal the future. Predictions others make about you may seem discouraging. The social or economic challenges you face may be daunting. Preconceptions you or others have about your family background may appear to limit you to some inherently negative predisposition. The great news is that all such challenges can be overcome by your choices.

Agency is the key that unlocks the pearly gates. We can choose to become joint heirs with the Savior. Through His holy prophets, He has made the doctrine clear. Here is Lehi's hopeful and inspiring declaration of our freedom to choose:

> All things have been done in the wisdom of him who knoweth all things. Adam fell that men might be; and men are, that they might have joy. And the Messiah cometh in the fullness of time, that he may redeem the children of men from the fall. And because that they are redeemed from the fall they have become free forever, knowing good from evil; to act for themselves and not to be acted upon, save it be by the punishment of the law at the great and last day,

according to the commandments which God hath given.

Wherefore, men are free according to the flesh; and all things are given them which are expedient unto man. And they are free to choose liberty and eternal life, through the great Mediator of all men, or to choose captivity and death, according to the captivity and power of the devil; for he seeketh that all men might be miserable like unto himself. And now, my sons, I would that ye should look to the great Mediator, and hearken unto his great commandments; and be faithful unto his words, and choose eternal life, according to the will of his Holy Spirit (2 Nephi 2:24–28).

Nowhere do the scriptures say we're all free to choose except for people who don't speak English. They don't say we're free to act for ourselves except those who don't have enough money or whose mother is a single parent. They don't say anywhere that agency is a gift from God that applies to all—except those who are depressed, whose fathers were drunks, or who couldn't get into BYU—or who believe they're not pretty, handsome, tall, smart, or thin enough.

We Can Always Choose

We're never without choice, no matter who we are or who our earthly parents are. Agency is a gift from our Heavenly Father, and He hopes we'll use it wisely.

Just as we're free to see the actions of our parents and model their behavior, so we're free to make the same observation and choose to act differently. We can choose to make our marriage celestial, or we can choose to ignore it completely.

Remember, improving our marriage is a team choice. Marriage is a joint venture. As we discussed earlier, we can control only our own behavior. So no one person can create a celestial relationship without the active participation of his or her partner.

The fact that each of us *can* choose is the principle to remember. Our Father in Heaven has bestowed this gift on us all. We get to choose how to respond to this world of ours. We have the power to overcome our amoebic instincts and conditioned responses.

REFRAMING

The way we see a picture can be greatly influenced by how that picture is displayed. The lighting, the location, and the frame can change how we view any image. The same is true of the situations we face in life. How we view the situations we encounter often depends on how they're presented.

We can change how we respond to something by changing how it's presented. In psychology or counseling, this is often referred to as *reframing*. By changing how a situation or concept is presented, we can often influence how we perceive it or respond to it.

This is also true in terms of how we see people, including ourselves. The labels we place on others and ourselves predispose us to see things in a certain way.

Similarly, the observations we receive through the media often color how we see the world.

How often have you heard labels like the following? Men are:

- pigs.
- stubborn.
- macho.
- arrogant.
- insensitive.
- selfish.
- immature.
- workaholics.
- lazy.

Now let's turn the tables. Women are:

- weepy.
- whiners.
- emotional.
- naggy.
- critical.
- ungrateful.
- gold-diggers.
- churchy.
- gossips.

Either list could go on much longer. It's interesting how the people who add to these lists toss out negative caricatures of the opposite sex. Those are the things they've been programmed to see when they look at others. Such a predisposition is a reflection of what they've been taught and what they've experienced. It's also a reflection of social reflex, a sort of negative political correctness that shows the battle of the sexes is still being fought and that we each have a side to support. Here's the party platform—close ranks and fire a volley at the other side.

Of course, this is counterproductive in promoting celestial understanding and harmony. The very things that are seen as undesirable in a mate can become assets if we are willing to frame the picture charitably. I'm not just talking rose-colored glasses here; I'm saying that, viewed in a more accepting way, what we're seeing might not be all bad.

LET'S TRY REFRAMING

Could "stubborn" actually be "persistent," for example? Or could "inflexible" be seen as "firm"? In that vein, consider some of the alternatives for the words below:

- lazy = calm, relaxed, unruffled.
- syrupy = kind.
- foolhardy = courageous.
- stubborn = persistent, perseverant.
- workaholic = good provider, ambitious, productive.
- unimaginative = practical, consistent, basic.
- weepy = sensitive, empathetic, emotionally involved.
- weak = gentle, kind, sensitive.
- boring = consistent, reliable.
- insensitive = emotionally consistent, unflappable.

- gossips = concerned, interested.
- angry = hurt, sad, lonely.

When we recognize that we can (to some extent) control how we see our spouse or ourselves, this gives us a bit of wiggle room so we can choose to be merciful and kind. We can develop charity and mercy in our relationships and hearts that we will appreciate in return.

In *The Merchant of Venice* (act 4, scene 1), Shakespeare describes the true nature of mercy, the effects of which ennoble any who are possessed of it:

> The quality of mercy is not strain'd,
>> It droppeth as the gentle rain from heaven
> Upon the place beneath: it's twice blest;
>> It blesseth him that gives and him that takes:
> 'Tis mightiest in the mightiest: it becomes
>> The throned monarch better than his crown;
> His sceptre shows the force of temporal power,
>> The attribute to awe and majesty,
> Wherein doth sit the dread and fear of kings;
>> But mercy is above this sceptred sway;
> It is enthroned in the hearts of kings,
>> It is an attribute to God himself;
> And earthly power doth then show likest God's
>> When mercy seasons justice.

A grandparent looking at the actions of a beloved grandchild sees the miracle, not the mess. With a heart predisposed to kindness, a grandma or grandpa often sees the exploration, not the explosion; the possibilities, not the past. Maybe that's why grandparents and grandchildren give and receive love so effortlessly. Both have the perspective to frame what they see lovingly. This kind predisposition costs nothing and may be the key to unlocking a loved one's heart.

When evaluating behavior—your spouse's or your own—don't forget that there's room to see what really exists. We have the tools to frame our lives and the lives of those we love in the most beautiful way possible.

Chapter 15

Listening

Do not weep; do not wax indignant. Understand.
— *Spinoza*

*O*ne of the most effective ways to demonstrate our respect for another person is by being interested in what that person says to us. Attentive listening demonstrates real interest.

Active listening is an art; it takes real commitment to master. Although our educational system is based in large part on our becoming successful listeners, the system dedicates little, if any, time to teaching us to truly listen.

There are some common problems that keep many of us from listening effectively. Here are some suggestions to help improve the quality of our listening skills.

Be Sure That You Can Hear

Make sure that you and your spouse have the physical capability to hear. This is the first and most fundamental of our listening suggestions.

A close friend told me he realized he had a problem when he spent half of the time in movies asking his wife what was being said. She suggested he have his hearing checked. At first he refused, insisting there was some Hollywood sound conspiracy and that, in other settings, he heard perfectly. But as he paid better attention to what he could and couldn't hear, my friend recognized he had a problem. He got his hearing checked; he now wears hearing aids and hears perfectly.

Unfortunately, many people refuse to be tested, even after a problem becomes evident. Hearing loss could mean we're old or broken, and vanity or arrogance keeps some of us from seeking help.

If you seem to be missing much of what's being said, even when you want to hear, perhaps there's a physical problem. Don't avoid help. The tests are painless, and you'll be glad you took the time.

Clear Your Heart

If you feel angry or frustrated or anxious, concentrating (and listening) can be difficult. It's hard to hear when emotions are running high. When you slow down as a speaker, you'll be better understood, and both sides of the conversation will generally change pace. Take a minute to slow down and set the stage so you can listen with purpose.

Say you've been stuck in traffic for the past twenty minutes. Perhaps right after you walk through the front door at home is not the time for your spouse to start a conversation about how to discipline your son or daughter. Ask for a minute to compose your heart, and shift from traffic to family mode.

Remember, if you use a line like "Give me a second to get my bearings," make sure you do come back to the requested topic. If you never seem to get ready to talk about those important issues, perhaps you're avoiding them by not preparing for meaningful communication. However, if you do take a minute and calmly prepare to be fully engaged in the conversation, that will go miles toward helping your partner see that you're interested and committed to better and more productive communication. And the next time you need a minute to compose yourself, your spouse will gladly give you the time you need, if that delay means getting you at your best and most responsive.

Listen to Everyone

We must consider every source of information if we're to get all the information we need. As Mark Twain said, "We're all ignorant, just on different subjects." The inverse is also true: "We all know something of value, just in different areas."

When we decide that a particular person or group

has nothing to say, we're eliminating a potential resource or opportunity. Not only that, we're sending a clear message to them: "You have nothing to say that I would value."

The general rule is that if you won't listen to me, I won't listen to you. Consider the saying "Children should be seen and not heard." If we hold this belief, our thought may be, "You kids go ahead and talk to me, but I'm going to read the paper."

Later, we're amazed that, as adolescents, these same kids don't want to talk to us. They fail to recognize the importance of what we want to say to them. They might not even believe us when we try to convince them of how important they are to us.

Perhaps in your employment history you recall a supervisor who acted as if he or she had nothing to learn from subordinates. If you had such a manager (and most of us have), I'm sure you remember how unimportant he or she made you feel.

I once heard a story about the unlikely contribution of an entry-level employee at a rural drug store. The employee suggested during a store meeting that the company provide double-print copies when film was brought in for photo processing. The employee commented that most people seemed to want to share their photos. Furthermore, the clerk suggested that there be no additional charge for the service.

Luckily the manager was interested enough to listen carefully, even though it was just an entry-level clerk doing the talking. Eventually that marketing strategy was implemented throughout the corporation and proved instrumental in building a small local retail group into a successful regional chain.

In short, the idea was worth millions.

DON'T ASSUME YOU KNOW WHAT'S COMING

Be patient enough not to jump ahead when someone is talking to you. Most of us are so interested in what we're going to say in reply that we spend our listening time composing our response. Maybe we want to sound bright, maybe we want to win an argument, or maybe we're just impatient, but we take the shortcut by assuming what will be said—and that means we're not listening.

My wife tests for this in the middle of a story by saying that my pants are on fire or that she knows how much I love fried Spam. When my response is, "That's nice, dear" or "Oh, that's interesting," I'm caught.

The solution is as simple as it is sometimes difficult. When someone is speaking to you, pay attention, listen, and then respond. They talk, you listen, then you respond, and they listen. Novel, but effective.

LISTEN WITHOUT SOLVING

The concept that listening should come before decision-making or advice-giving is foreign to some people. An even more radical idea is that a person might want only a listening ear, not a problem-solving consultant.

There are two important traps to avoid here. First, make sure you have all the information you need (or the speaker wishes to share) before rendering an opinion. Second, confirm that your spouse, or whomever you're listening to, actually *wants* an opinion from you—before you give one. Either way, the key is getting the message before you respond. Then be thoughtful, using all your skill and experience to address the issue. Being asked for help is a wonderful compliment that should not be taken lightly.

An acquaintance recently told me she was so grateful when a friend sat patiently and listened to her "date from heck" experience—especially when the listener did not follow it up with her own worst-date-ever story. What if the friend, rather than listening and responding with care and interest, had said, "You think that's bad, wait till you hear this one!" She would have gone from interested confidante to the *Can You Top This?* game-show host.

A single sister told me of her first contact with her bishop after moving into a new ward. She reported, "I knew right away I would like him. He was the first bishop I had shared my feelings with who didn't begin his response by saying, 'I know exactly how you feel.' Instead, he began with, 'That must be very difficult for you. I'm sorry you've had to go through that.'" Even though many of us might think we know how the other is feeling, it's nice to feel that we were listened to.

LISTEN FOR CONTEXT AS WELL AS CONTENT

Emotions, needs, and feelings are part of the message being sent, sometimes a critical part. This is especially true when the message comes from someone close to you.

One of the best examples of this kind of message is the instantaneous and timely anger of a child. In an effort to express the frustration and anger of the moment, a child often overreacts. Saying "I hate you!" is a common way for a child to lash out. Obviously the child who explodes like this doesn't really hate Mom or Dad. Rather, the child is expressing anger about something he or she somehow connects to Mom or Dad.

Perhaps the only reason the focus is on Mom or Dad is that they happen to be there at the moment when frustration boils over. Many times the real source of sadness, anger, or frustration is not to be found in the first message we hear; we just happen to be there when the pot boils over.

Have you ever heard these kinds of apologetic disclaimers?

- "Sorry, I didn't mean that. It's just been a rough week."
- "I don't know what's wrong with me. Sorry."
- "I'm sorry—it's not you, it's me."

If the message you're getting from your spouse seems overly emotional or more negative than fits the situation, be mindful that the context of your partner's message might be coming through more effectively than the content. What's being felt is coloring the message. This is a good time to remind yourself that one answer to the question that's popping into your mind—"What did I do to deserve this?"—might be, "Nothing."

This is the time we need to provide a stable and sensitive listening ear. It's not a time to get defensive or combative. Sometimes the kindest and most effective listening technique of all is just to be there.

CHAPTER 16

Solving Problems

The measure of success is not whether you have a tough problem to deal with,
but whether it's the same problem you had to deal with last year.

—*John Foster Dulles*

Solving problems is something we do all the time. But most of us, busy as we are, tend to react to problems rather than anticipate and prevent them. In addition, few couples work on solving problems together. For many, it's hard enough just to find time together to communicate, let alone address problems.

The problem-solving process and the decision-making that follows are key elements in planning our lives. The problem-solving process is simple. But like any process that requires change, it can still be difficult to do.

Whenever we deal with change, there's that rule of thumb (in chapter 3) that reminds us of the potential difficulty. Remember? "No change in the universe takes place without movement. No movement occurs without friction. No friction happens without heat."

Any change, even in the smallest amount, can generate an uncomfortable amount of heat. Some of us instinctively avoid the inevitable heat of change in spite of the pain of the status quo. We choose the pain we know over the pain we don't know. What we often fail to understand is that, if handled wisely, change doesn't have to be painful; in fact, it may even be pleasant.

START WITH SOME BASIC AGREEMENT

As with questioning and other communication skills, solving problems effectively requires that you and your spouse agree on some basic assumptions. This will help avoid needless hurt and confusion. The same rules we established for questioning apply here, as well as these others to consider:

- Every problem is our problem (not your problem or my problem).
- We'll focus on solutions, not fault. (In describing the problem, we may discover that one spouse's actions have contributed to the problem.)
- We all make mistakes or poor decisions based on bad information or assumptions. (Recognize that the focus of problem-solving is not incrimination or punishment for past behavior but improving the situation.)
- Solutions often take time. (Patience during the trial-

and-error of problem-solving is one of the keys to success.)

With those additional rules, here are four skills needed in effective problem-solving:

1. *Describe the current situation.* (What's happening now? What does the status quo look like?) This can be a written description or a discussion. The idea is to describe what is currently happening that's causing problems. Be as specific as you can without being combative or hurtful.

2. *Describe the ideal outcome.* (What do you want to happen? What would ideal look like? This is not a description of perfection but of what is reasonable and possible given the situation.) This can be a written description or a discussion of what you would like to see in place of what is currently happening. Again, be as clear and specific as you can. We generally know the outcome we'd like to see. An excellent therapist and mentor suggested to me one of the most valuable questions we can ask clients as counseling begins: "What would it look like if you were well?" Somewhere in our hearts or souls we know what needs to change in our lives. We know how we want things to be. I've used this question many times, with great success.

The therapist told me that often his clients would answer the question with "I don't know." He suggested a follow-up question to that response: "If you did know, what would it look like?" My experience has been the same as his: Every one of those people who've said they didn't know had no trouble answering the second question, once asked. We know better than anyone else what we would like to see change in our lives. The challenge is to take the time, and be brave enough, to describe just how we want our lives to be. If we don't, getting where we want to go becomes almost impossible.

3. *Compare the current situation with the ideal.* (List the differences. What needs to be added? What needs to stop? What resources are available?) Change means adding or deleting. The simplicity of this may be hard to see at first. But as you identify the things you want to see happen, you'll find the concept easy to apply. Just compare the two descriptions you've created—the current situation and the ideal one. What are the differences in the two? Those differences will come down to what we need to get rid of and what we need to add. Develop a brief outline of who does what, when, where, and how to add the needed components and dump the unwanted ones.

4. *Implement changes.* (Create a plan of action for everything that needs to be added or deleted. Who? What? Where? When? How?) Let's say you want to start a weekly planning meeting. You have described the problem in doing so as having too many schedule conflicts and using time ineffectively. After comparing how things are with how you want them to be, you might come up with a plan like this: "We will meet Sunday night at 8:00 P.M. for a half hour to coordinate our weekly schedules. I will get the information from the kids on

what they need to do this week. You will bring the desk calendar, and we will coordinate it with my office schedule and your pocket scheduler. We will try this for three weeks, evaluate the results, and make adjustments as needed."

After you've developed a brief outline of who does what, when, where, and how, take one step at a time to make the required changes. If you don't stop or are not turned aside, you'll end up where you want to be. The truth is as simple as compound interest. Time, patience, and consistency are the greatest factors in the completion of any task.

Exercise: Try Solving a Problem

Choose a problem you would like to solve and apply the four steps of problem-solving:

1. Describe the current situation.
2. Describe the ideal outcome.
3. Compare the current situation with the ideal.
4. Make the necessary changes.

One important note: We must recognize that we all have limited resources. There's just so much time, money, and energy available. And that is why we begin by seeking for improvement, not perfection.

It's also valuable to remember that we can't change anyone but ourselves. That's why we're looking for the

ideal solution—not the perfect solution—to our difficul-
ties. Even so, there's almost no situation that can't be
improved with goodwill and cooperation.

CHAPTER 17

Cultivating Fascination

The universe is full of magical things, patiently waiting for our wits to grow sharper.
—Eden Phillpotts

How do we learn to appreciate who we are? What keeps us excited about learning? Observation has convinced me that adults compulsively try to make learning into work. We sit and brainstorm, we study, and we make lists. We create task forces and committees.

This is true in counseling, too. Many couples start off with a misconception that makes success harder than it has to be, and perhaps impossible for some. The misconception is that "the relationship" is some independent life form separate from the people in it. Further, they think doing something to make it better has to be unpleasant.

That doesn't sound very appealing, does it? When

you fell in love, was it work? Was it the relationship itself that you couldn't live without, that you ached to hold and be with? I don't think so. You love each other; you don't love the relationship.

Somehow, at some point, life became a compartment, not a vista. We learned to define ourselves by the tasks we do, and one of those tasks became the relationship. Somehow, along the way, the marriage became just another job. Does our daily to-do list read like this?

- Attend PTA meeting.
- Clean toilets.
- Take watch to be fixed.
- Work on "the relationship."

Remember how you first found out about the person you married? Most likely you were immersed in the thoughts of this person. You couldn't wait to see the person again, and you were more than happy to talk about anything at all that helped you know him or her better.

How about trying that now? Can you pause a moment in reading today's newspaper to be really interested in what your spouse has to tell you?

NATURAL INTEREST

The quickest learners on the planet are children. That's partly because of the natural condition of their brains and the developmental stages that predispose them to experiment. By watching them, though, you can discover the real secret. They never work at learning. They're simply fascinated by life. They immerse themselves in everything they do. Everything is an adventure to be savored in the moment.

That's how we learned about our husbands and wives. We were honestly interested to the point of fascination. No fact about them was too trivial. None of their thoughts or feelings were unimportant. We really wanted to be a part of everything that had to do with them.

It's important to remember that there's an eternity of interest ahead, if we choose to be interested. But we need a shift in our thinking. We need to remember that our relationship is not just another job. The relationship is between our spouse and us—not some third party. It's life. It's why we came here.

BEING PRESENT

"Being present" means giving time and accepting time as a gift from your mate. Being present in your relationship is as significant as it is simple. It's a two-part concept that will change your life as you put it into practice.

First, if you want a relationship, it will require time together. Second, a successful relationship requires that when you're together you really need to *be* there, to be fully present.

Many adults have experienced talking to a child while doing something else, reading the paper or watching TV. The child will seldom accept this divided attention. One day my daughter climbed onto my lap, brushed the newspaper aside, grabbed me by both ears, and said,

"Daddy, look at me!" She wanted me to be *present* when we talked, not just there in body. She wanted me fully engaged: body, mind, and spirit.

Time together means just that. The amount of time you spend together is a real factor in whether you're building the relationship you're capable of building.

Marriage is the joining of two distinct individuals. It was never intended to erase the individual or make one spouse subservient to the other. Rather, it should enhance their opportunity to have an abundant and joyful eternity together. There needs to be a balance in our lives that reflects attention to every valuable aspect of who we are and what we do. Church callings, employment, community involvement, activities with the children, hobbies, personal relaxation, and education are all parts of a full and joyful life.

However, the key word here is *balance*. How you spend your time should reflect how much you value each of these worthy activities.

We're not stupid. We know whether the time we spend building an eternal companionship is commensurate with its value. There are code words and phrases of all kinds that reflect our guilt or rationale for not spending the time we know is required. Our use of these words indicates that we already know we need more time together—for example, "I'm working all these extra hours so that when we do have time together, it will be quality time."

What are the implications of the code words "quality

time"? For the most part, they mean "more money." That's why you're working more hours. They could also mean "more toys." The implication is that time together without more money or more toys is not quality time. Working more hours could also indicate a desire to have more prestige or power at work. The implication is that more power at work is more valuable than our presence at home.

Another example might be, "I need some time for me." That could be the absolute truth; time for personal activities can be critical. But when applied to our time together, those words could mean, "There's nothing else in my life that's less valuable than my time with you. In other words, the only thing I can cut back on to find some personal time is our time together."

Obviously there's a problem when we look at it in those terms. The real question is, does how you spend your time accurately reflect what's truly valuable to you? It's time to grow up and recognize that no one has time to do every good thing available. So we must choose where and how our time is most wisely and enjoyably spent. Perspective (preferably eternal) plus effective and efficient coordination of our time are the things that are needed in making the right choices.

What Matters Most

Several years ago a close friend, Bill, had a life-changing experience. He had trained for months to participate in a long-distance bicycle ride. The event was for charity, and he had sponsors lined up to donate for both distance and time. He had trained hard and was in remarkable physical shape.

On the morning of the ride, as he prepared to leave the house and ride to the starting area, Bill became ill. He felt dizzy and faint. He fell as he tried to get on his bike. Bill's girlfriend heard the noise and came in to find him flat on the ground, unable to stand. She called 911 and tried to provide some comfort.

He later told me his equilibrium was so affected that he was sure they had put him on the wall rather than the floor of the ambulance. On the way to the hospital he became unconscious.

Bill had experienced a small aneurysm in his brain. But that medical fact is not as important as the experience itself, from Bill's perspective. While he was unconscious, he had a typical near-death experience.

That's not all. During this time of extreme medical emergency, his doctors decided they needed to limit the stimuli to his brain. They restrained him, covered his eyes and ears, and kept him in almost total silence. They had to wait several days for the fluid around the aneurysm to clear before they could scan the area and accurately assess the damage.

In the meantime, Bill regained consciousness. He was sedated and had no memory after being put into the ambulance. Considering his condition, restrained in the silent darkness, Bill assumed he must be dead and in hell. He began to despair, and he searched his life for what he'd done to deserve this.

Bill is not a member of the Church and had little background in theology. What he did know is that he was where he was, and he wanted to know why. He reviewed his life and wished desperately that he could change some things. Whether from the medication, the injury, or sensory deprivation, he began to hallucinate. He heard voices, saw visions, heard choirs, and reviewed his life over and over again.

Eventually he awoke and recovered fully. The change in his life was profound. He married his longtime girl-friend in a matter of weeks, committed to cherish her every day, and has. He changed how he related to his customers; he spent less time worrying about money and more time being concerned with the people in his life. Interestingly, his business boomed, and he made time to branch into more creative endeavors.

When I asked him what had changed the most for him, his answer came without hesitation: "I enjoy every moment of every day. I love my family and friends and remember that nothing we can do in life is more impor-tant than the people we love."

My friend Bill changed his life many years ago, and the change has been sustained. He is as happy, caring, and warm a person as I know. When you're with him, you know that he really cares about you and the time you're spending together. He's learned how to give the gift of his time and accept the gift of yours. He's learned how to be engaged in living the moment. He's learned how to be present in his relationships—for all the right reasons.

PAY ATTENTION

Can you tell if someone you're with is really interested in being there? Of course you can. So can your spouse. It's not just your physical proximity that those who love you are after; it's also your presence in the present. Effective listening and communication are a natural extension of our willingness and commitment to be present.

Earlier I mentioned quality time. The gift you give to others by being fully engaged when you're with them is the gift of quality time. What you're giving is yourself. That doesn't mean you need to become subservient to those around you, becoming a human lapdog waiting patiently on the will of your masters. It just means that when you spend time with someone, you should be there. Express yourself, interact, be you, fully engaged and involved, getting the most out of every interaction and experience. Find ways to value the precious time you're sharing and care about the person you're spending it with. Learn how to give the gift of your time and accept the gift of theirs. Learn how to be engaged in living the moment. Learn how, for all the right reasons, to be present in your relationships.

WE NEED TOUCH

Learning to accept touch and learning to touch lovingly are important aspects of being together. Appropriate

physical contact with your spouse runs the entire spectrum of positive touch, from sexual intimacy to the comfort of a reassuring pat on the back. The desire to be close
physically is an extension of our emotional bond, our
desire to be close emotionally.

How close you sit, when you're free to choose, is
often a barometer of how well your relationship is doing.
Many marriage counselors have several seating arrange-
ments in their offices, and they note carefully where a
couple chooses to sit relative to each other. Holding
hands, walking arm in arm, or having your arm around
your partner as you walk or sit are all expressions of
commitment and connection.

We need the constant reassurance and comfort of contact. When we discuss or plan or communicate, part of
the message we send is nonverbal. To improve the
impact of our exchanges, we need to improve the nonverbal messages as well.

Touch often as you speak or listen. When you meet,
share a hug and kiss as part of your greeting, if appropriate. Be open in your excitement and fondness to be
together. An example is the moments you've observed at
airports or train stations as you've glimpsed moments of
greeting and farewell. I don't mean those overly syrupy
or inappropriately dramatic moments; I mean the observable reunion of hearts coming together. The exuberant
smile, the welcoming hug, the eye contact that holds
unspoken energy—these are the things that say, "I love
you, I missed you, and I'm glad we're together."

Every time we touch, there's that same opportunity to convey how we feel, to reassure, to comfort, to connect. In a world that seems designed to isolate and insulate us from each other, the loving contact of your spouse is the beacon on a foggy night that God intended to guide us home.

And why not? The image Michelangelo used in the Sistine Chapel to convey the eternal connection between God and humanity is—what else? A touch.

The comfort and confidence of being connected to another is emotional armor in our daily battle. We need and want the touchstone of loving connection. Resolve in your marriage to provide and accept it, and enjoy the blessings of being together.

CHAPTER 18

Finding Out What Makes You Feel Loved

A high degree of empathy in a relationship is possibly the most potent
factor in bringing about change and learning.

—Carl Rogers

For our anniversary one year, I decided I could best show my true feelings for my wife, Lois, by giving her a pair of chest waders. I pictured her in the waders—neoprene, blue, and wonderful—sharing the experience of fishing with me, her true and eternal companion, on a remote Alaskan trout stream.

I saw her warm and comfortable in spite of the weather. In the theater of my mind, she smiled and waved as she landed yet another monster trout. She knew in her heart that these expensive waders allowed her to enjoy being with me. She was warm and comfortable, despite weather that I envisioned deteriorating in

176

typical Alaskan fall fashion. Oh, how grateful she was for the gift and my concern for her comfort!

It turned out that I was right: Lois loved the waders! We've enjoyed the experience of fishing and sharing the outdoors together many times since I gave her that gift. She never forgets to mention that being warm makes all the difference in how she experiences the day's fishing. She loves the outdoors and is good at fly-fishing, but she hates to be cold. Oh, how wonderful those waders have been!

Would it surprise you to know that my daughters—upon first hearing my plans to give my sweet bride waders for our anniversary—were skeptical? They suggested that I was out of touch with reality, and they were quite convincing. I confess (in a moment of self-doubt) that I faltered, purchased Lois's favorite perfume, and held it in "Of-course-I-was-just-kidding-I'm-not-that-insensitive-you-know" reserve.

The point is, sometimes we're right about how the things we do affect our spouse's feelings, and sometimes we're not. We often assume and leave it at that. We might find, however, that what we feel is undeniable evidence of our love is not always seen that way by our spouse.

How Do We Feel Love?

There are two questions that do a good job of helping us discover what we do to show love, and what we feel as love.

The first question is, "What do I do to show you my

love?" This lets us share perceptions of the actions we intend as loving.

The second question is, "What do you do that I feel demonstrates your love for me?" This question gives feedback about what our mate perceives as loving.

It may surprise you to learn what your mate is doing as a way to show love. It may also surprise you to find out what you do that is appreciated. These may be things you didn't realize were as important to your spouse as they are.

A friend shared with me how much he was touched by the simplest action of his wife. At a New Year's Eve party, she put her arm around him as they stood together talking with friends. This is a longtime marriage. These are people who love each other. Even so, this simple action was a much-appreciated gift. It demonstrated to the husband his wife's love for him. By telling her later how he felt, he showed his appreciation, but he also helped her learn how she might demonstrate her feelings effectively in the future.

Whenever your spouse does something that you appreciate, *be appreciative*. Gratitude is the heart of reward in relationships—and in life, for that matter. Being thankful and expressing it educates and rewards your spouse for doing good things. If something your spouse does brings you positive feelings, tell him or her. This recognition and communication will help your spouse feel great. At the same time, it will help you recognize that your spouse wants you to feel great too.

Exercise: Find Out What to Do

Take time to respond to these two questions by making a brief list of your responses.

First question: "What do I do to show you my love?"

Some responses might be:

- I keep the yard clean.
- I go to movies that you want to see.
- I respect your opinion and ask for advice.
- I bring you flowers and cards to let you know I'm thinking of you.
- I call when I'm out of town because I miss you.
- I'm kind and loving to your parents and siblings because I know you love them.
- I want to spend time with you.
- I care about what you think, so we talk about the things around us.
- I admire you as a parent, so I try to work with you in raising our kids.
- I compliment you often.
- I appreciate your hard work.
- I love to be close to you and enjoy our intimate time together.

Second question: "What do you do that I feel shows your love for me?"

Some responses might be:

- You help me whenever I ask.
- You listen to my explanation of how my day went.

- You cuddle.
- You work hard to provide for our family.
- You listen intently and are genuinely interested in what I do, and in me.
- You let me pick the radio station in the car.
- You turn off the radio when we drive so we can talk.

Your lists aren't intended to be complete. If someone forgets something, that's okay. What we're trying to do is share and learn, not reestablish the inquisition!

Write down your complete list of answers to the questions first; then discuss them. Take turns sharing one thing from one spouse's list, then one from the other.

Finish both lists of answers to the first question before going on. That means that if one list has more items than the other, one spouse might have to finish by reading several items in a row. When the first question is answered and both lists are exhausted, go on to the second.

This is a time to be grateful. When giving or getting answers, assume that your spouse is being honest. So, be honest—but gentle. "You can't possibly believe I think you love me when you do that" is not the kind of response that would be productive.

HOW ARE YOU DOING?

The real intent of having the discussion in the exercise above is to clarify which of our actions are effective in demonstrating love for our spouse. The exercise also allows us to better understand the intentions of our partner's heart. Something we hardly notice can be a real effort by our mate to demonstrate love. For example, consider the husband who feels that going to work every day demonstrates his love. Often in counseling, when a husband is asked by his wife if he really loves her, his response is, "I go to work every day, don't I?" His spouse often overlooks this demonstration of love on the husband's part because she has not considered his going to work as an act of love. What the act is doesn't matter as much as recognizing the condition of the giver's heart.

It's always worth the effort to show your recognition of your spouse's efforts to show love. Listing these actions—as you did in the exercise—provides an opportunity to feel appreciated. Being thanked and thankful are wonderful elixirs for the soul, and they provide building blocks for real growth.

CHAPTER 19

Enjoying the Process

This is the day which the Lord hath made; we will rejoice and be glad in it.
—Psalm 118:24

Our culture tends to measure success by the worldly goods and services we produce, or by how much worldly power we have. The other aspects of our lives are mostly unheralded and ignored. The things we have that set us above others are recognized so much more than who we are. Those things have practically come to define the individual in our society. Most of us get carried away with what we have and how to measure it, and somehow along the way we lose the bigger picture.

If we stopped even for a moment to consider how misguided or misplaced our values have become in the worldly economy, the foolishness of it would become obvious. Power, money, and fame are the coin of the realm. How far or straight we can hit a golf ball has become more important than how honest we are or how much we love our families. How we look in our costly raiment has become more important to our success than the content of our hearts.

What we should honor is charity, kindness, courage, integrity, wisdom, loyalty, and the other human attributes that add real value to the world. What we should be measuring and treasuring is the content of our character, not how we look. We should value substance over appearance. Unfortunately, the prestige of where we end up has become the important thing, not how we got there or who we've become when we arrive.

THE GOAL INCLUDES THE PROCESS

This goal-driven existence misses the point of life. We learn, love, have joy, grow, and exist in the process. Life is the day-by-day expression of what we are up to that point, and where we intend to go. Growth or gain is measurable and experienced only in relation to where we are, where we've been, and where we're going.

Do you recognize a theme here? We live in a society that confuses the destination with the journey. Worse yet, the destinations we seek are often not those of celestial importance. Thus we've become a people who will be happy only when we reach some material goal. We've devalued the process of reaching the objective to the point that we consider the daily journey called life as

valueless and mundane. This process—this worldly con-
ditioning—starts early and stays with us, limiting the
appreciation we feel in every stage of our lives.

Does any of this sound familiar? I'll be happy:

- when I can start school and be like the big kids.
- when I'm tall enough to go on the big rides at the park.
- when I get a new bike and summer won't be so boring.
- when I get to high school and the real fun begins.
- when I'm old enough to date—life will be good!
- when someone asks me to the prom (I'll know I'm a success then).
- when I get my first job so I have the money I need.
- when I get married and I'm free of the rules of this house.
- when I get the right education and I'm able to succeed; that diploma is my ticket to success.
- when the kids start school, because then I'll be able to do what I want.
- when I get a real job that gives me a raise; then we can do some great things.
- when we get that cabin and have some fun weekends.
- when they put me in charge; then things will change.
- when our house is paid for, because then we can do some really enjoyable things.
- when the kids move away for good.
- when I retire—that's when the fun begins.

I'm not saying achievement is valueless. But achievement can be appreciated fully only if the process of achieving has also been appreciated. If the outcome of a good, moral, and joyful journey is fame and gold, all the better. But the undeniable truth is, we need to enjoy and celebrate the journey.

Exercise: Stop and Discover the Joy

When we're all so busy looking toward the ever-changing goal, we miss the potential joy of the journey. Here are some questions we could ask, and should if we want to discover this potential joy:

- What is there about today to enjoy?
- How am I blessed?
- What am I learning?
- How have I grown in my life?
- What have I learned from my children?
- Whom have I loved over the years, and what has that taught me?

The point of this discussion is to look for the things of value today, or up until now. The future is bright and may hold countless joys. So does today.

WHAT WE GAIN BY LIVING

Life is about what we gain from the experience of living, start to finish. We can reflect back on the whole process, learn from it, and enjoy the memory of it. We accept this in some areas of our experience quite easily. Take, for example, a concert. Your favorite group sings or plays songs you've heard before. As you listen, do you say to yourself, "I wish this were over. Then I could say I experienced the concert. Gee, would that be great."

It's not like that at all. We anticipate the experience in advance. We enjoy the concert itself. Then we appreciate the memory of it. There's an opportunity to enjoy the process of the concert from start to finish and beyond.

The same can be said for planning, experiencing, and recalling a vacation. Some of the most fun I ever have comes simply from remembering a fishing trip or anticipating the next one. Does that sound familiar to you? As you think back on some notable experiences in your life, can you recall those moments of anticipation beforehand and fond memories after?

This sense of appreciation differs from experience to experience. It's certainly easier to see when we talk about enjoyable things in life than when discussing the difficult or challenging experiences we encounter. We seem to recognize the value of the hard experiences more easily in retrospect. When we're in the midst of a challenge, it's difficult to see the possible positive things the experience might provide. But if we understand that we can learn something from the tough times, we may at least have a sliver of hope during those challenges.

CELEBRATE OR CONTEMPLATE

Basketball coach John Wooden said, "When you win, you celebrate. When you lose, you contemplate. When do you learn?"

This thought shows a clear understanding of the long-term value of learning from our mistakes and challenges. If you asked Coach Wooden how much he liked to lose, what do you suppose he'd say? Sure, he prefers winning—who doesn't?

But the truth is, sometimes we lose. Sometimes we make mistakes. The real question is how we handle them and learn from them. We must learn to accept the good and bad things in life as parts of the whole. If we're going to be successful at life, we must accept the fact that the good and bad are up to us to manage and to learn from. And we must remember that the same is true of marriage.

Have you ever played Scrabble? It's a board game in which you draw letters to make words in crossword-puzzle fashion. Each player picks letters blindly, through the luck of the draw. But if you've chosen to play the game, you've also consented to take the letters you draw and do the best you can with them.

Life provides a similar challenge. We don't always have the experiences we'd choose to have. We're given a certain set of circumstances. How we deal with them is the measure of our success.

We each have different talents, skills, experiences, and opportunities. Some have wealth given them at birth.

These winners of the gene-pool lottery are lucky. I congratulate them.

Some of us were not so blessed in that area. Perhaps our gift at birth was of faith or music or intelligence. We're lucky too. I congratulate us, too.

The question is not whether we received gifts at birth to help us with the journey that is life, for each of us did. Each of us has been given, by God, the gifts we need to help us: "And all these gifts come by the Spirit of Christ; and they come unto every man severally, according as he will. And I would exhort you, my beloved brethren, that ye remember that every good gift cometh of Christ" (Moroni 10:17–18).

What to Do with God's Gifts to Us

What to do with these gifts is the question we must ask ourselves every day. How do we apply our time, talents, and energies to life? As always, it's up to us. Every day is a mix of the good and bad life dishes out. What we choose to do with it, when, how, and with whom, is the fabric of our lives.

Our choices define what we really produce. That product is living, what we do with the time and opportunity God has given us. The challenge is to live fully in real time without losing the joy of good memories or the education of painful experience. We do that by recognizing the potential of great dreams and the power of appropriate goals without forgetting that today is how we get there.

I believe that when we leave this world, we take only two things with us: what we learned and whom we loved. It only makes sense, then, that our daily existence should focus on loving and learning. In the end, that combination is the investment that pays the real dividend.

If we have learned to be happily married, it will be because our focus truly was on learning and loving. When that is so, the possibilities are truly endless. In fact, they are eternal!

Index